"If we too are to wa ... , it
is imperative to rer ... h-
lin has most articul ... ho
serve and hold the l

Dr. Lance Plyler, Director, World Medical Mission,
a ministry of Samaritan's Purse

"*Promises in the Dark* provides a transparent account of the arduous and sometimes even despairing work of medical missions in the field. McLaughlin wrestles with questions of theodicy in this book in the context of extreme poverty and disease in developing nations, and he finds hope and solace in a return to the promises of God in life and love. This book is not for the faint of heart."
Jenny Eaton Dyer, Founder, The 2030 Collaborative

"To serve and live among the poor is not an easy road. It's a walk with suffering and slow, small victories. McLaughlin and his brave community of doctors have willfully brought their families behind the dark curtain of poverty in one of the poorest corners on earth. McLaughlin shows us how the burden of knowledge and conviction are gifts not to be wasted. God's promises of faith, hope, and love far outweigh the doubts and disappointments."
Brandon Heath, GRAMMY®-nominated, Dove Award–winning recording artist

"Ministry to those who acutely experience sin's effects in this world leads many Christians to reconsider their calling. For those at risk of having compassion and optimism replaced by despair and cynicism, Eric McLaughlin offers much-needed hope. This hope is anchored in the promises and character of God himself. The reader will not only empathize with Eric's honest confessions, but identify how they too can actuate these life-giving Truths."
Mark Tatlock, President, The Master's Academy International

"I had to stop repeatedly, often in tears, to respond to what God stirred in my heart as I read Eric's articulate account of life in an African hospital where many die, often after much prayer for healing. These experiences kept bringing Eric back to God's suffering Redeemer Son Jesus, and this book will call you to do the same when you don't understand the suffering around you."

Don Finto, Author; Pastor Emeritus, Belmont Church, Nashville; founder, Caleb Company

"As a missionary coworker of Eric's for two years in Kenya, I attest that these 'promises in the dark' arise from the heart of a humble servant of Christ whom God has gifted with profound insight for the challenges faced in caring for the sick and dying without losing hope. Each chapter, and the discussion questions that follow, will serve as powerful tools for personal or group discipleship."

Dr. Mike Chupp, Chief Executive Officer, Christian Medical and Dental Associations

"Real, honest, vulnerable, and with a depth that strikes the core is how I would describe this book. If you have served in areas of need, you can relate to each story. It gives opportunity for discussions on very pertinent issues, and maybe as we face the uncertainties and many questions with openness shall we turn to the Author and Perfecter of our faith."

Dr. Matilda Ong'ondi, Physician and clinical hemato-oncologist, Kenya

"There are many books exhorting Christians to go and serve the Lord in cross-cultural contexts, but few that are meant to be read while wrestling through the sorrows and struggles they'll encounter in those situations. Eric McLaughlin has written such a book, indispensable for all who feel the pain of death and suffering in their day-to-day work."

Dr. Matthew Loftus, Missionary physician in Kenya; writer at MereOrthodoxy.com

"*Promises in the Dark* is a warm lamplight to accompany pilgrims whose progress has been dampened by the doubt and discouragement that often pervade those who live amid scenes of persisting darkness. These words can give even the weariest of souls the courage to utter once more, 'Your kingdom come, your will be done, on earth as it is in heaven.'"

Andrew Greer, Dove Award–nominated singer-songwriter; author; television host of the Amazon Prime show *Dinner Conversations with Mark Lowry and Andrew Greer*

"*Promises in the Dark* is a profound, realistic, and thought-provoking book that offers insight into the daily struggles of a missionary doctor serving disadvantaged populations. There is a shining light amidst darkness of insufficiency, despair, and hopelessness in the loving sacrifice and mercy of our Savior Jesus, who has called us to his labor. I recommend it to every coworker in the front lines of Christian service."

Dr. Castro Mugalla, Family Physician, Iten County Referral Hospital, Iten, Kenya

"Eric McLaughlin, a missionary physician, engages the raw and compelling questions of what it means to be human and trust God in the face of a world that is stark and at times cruel. Eric offers no simple answers or trite truisms. Instead, he invites us to engage the questions with the confidence that there is nothing we face that Jesus has not first entered. There is something about life and love that lingers far longer than heartache, and it is this story that enables us to enter all other losses with hope. This book will intensify your passion and encourage you to live the best story ever told."

Dan B. Allender, Professor of Counseling Psychology and Founding President, The Seattle School of Theology and Psychology

"As a pastor, friend, and family member, I've walked in many stories of brokenness, illness, and loss which have left me feeling overwhelmed and helpless, and frustrated because I couldn't fix things. I came away from Eric's book realizing, once again, that God's promises claim us more than we claim them. The pressure is off. We're called to be servant-lovers, not omnicompetent-fixers. Hope is certain because of Jesus's resurrection and return, but life between those glorious markers is anything but predictable and controllable. This book will be an invaluable guide for many who are tired of empty clichés and baseless formulas and long for honest reflections and encouragement for loving well, even when the healing doesn't come."

Scotty Smith, Pastor Emeritus, Christ Community Church, Franklin, TN; teacher in residence, West End Community Church, Nashville, TN

"Eric McLaughlin brought me to tears with this honest look at the difficulties of the life of a compassionate caregiver. When dealing with this broken world, there are no simple answers. But there can be hope. *Promises in the Dark* is essential reading for anyone who walks with others through suffering and questions how to keep on going."

Dr. Kent Brantly, Ebola survivor; coauthor of *Called for Life*

"What does a lived-out faith look like in the throes of an African field hospital? In a world of disease, death, and brokenness—of broken promises—how does one live as a light to the world? The answers to these questions are to be found in the pages of this honest book."

Michael Card, Songwriter; Bible teacher

"If you, like me, deal with needy people, demanding family situations, or challenging circumstances, this book is for you. With riveting stories and enlightening insights, this book will help you find the path to perseverance, hope, and even joy! I love this book and will be recommending it to everyone I know."

Dr. David Stevens, CEO Emeritus, Christian Medical & Dental Associations; author of *Jesus, M.D.*

Promises
in the Dark

Walking with Those in Need
Without Losing Heart

Eric McLaughlin

New
Growth
Press
WWW.NEWGROWTHPRESS.COM

New Growth Press, Greensboro, NC 27404
newgrowthpress.com
Copyright © 2019 by Eric McLaughlin

Cover Design: Faceout Books, faceoutstudio.com
Interior Typesetting and eBook: lparnellbookservices.com

ISBN: 978-1-64507-029-0 (Print)
ISBN: 978-1-64507-054-2 (eBook)

Library of Congress Cataloging-in-Publication Data
Names: McLaughlin, Eric, author.
Title: Promises in the dark : walking with those in need without losing
    heart / Eric McLaughlin.
Description: Greensboro : New Growth Press, 2019. | Includes bibliographical
    references.
Identifiers: LCCN 2019019590 (print) | ISBN 9781645070290 (trade paper)
Subjects: LCSH: Caring—Religious aspects—Christianity. | Caregivers—
    Religious life.
Classification: LCC BV4647.S9 M35 2019 (print) | LCC BV4647.S9 (ebook) |
    DDC 259/.4—dc23
LC record available at https://lccn.loc.gov/2019019590
LC ebook record available at https://lccn.loc.gov/2019980106

Printed in the United States of America

27 26 25 24 23 22 21 20   3 4 5 6 7

CONTENTS

This is my comfort in my affliction,
that your promise gives me life.

PSALM 119:50

Introduction

～

Over the last nine years, the life God has given me has tossed my heart in every known direction. I have been crushed. I have rejoiced. I have been sometimes overwhelmed and sometimes bored. I have been astounded both by the badness of the bad and the goodness of the good. I have known despair and hope and every variegation in between. There is always struggle, and sometimes there is resolution. I have often wondered if I can keep going. I have wondered what will become of me if I do.

From the beginning of our medical careers and our relationship with each other, my wife Rachel and I had been committed to working internationally as missionaries among medically underserved people. For me, there was no big flash of special calling, other than the general calling to glorify God with the gifts he has given me in service of the world he loves. Then, in 2007, when Rachel and I were nearing the end of our medical residencies (Obstetrics/Gynecology and Family Practice, respectively), we were approached by two other families about the possibility of pursuing long-term medical work in Africa together as a community of families. At that time, the importance of having a close community amid the daily challenges of a sometimes-isolated missionary life was looming large for us, and we had already known these friends for several years. As we prayed and talked further, we all concluded that the opportunity to merge our three life stories was more than mere coincidence but contained something of the compelling, albeit always mysterious, call of God.

In 2009, we all moved to rural Kenya for two years to learn African medicine and seek a place where our small community of families could invest long-term in serving people who otherwise had little or no access to medical care. We also wanted to train and disciple African doctors who could take their gifts throughout their home countries. We found such a place in the interior of Burundi, a small East African nation which is arguably the poorest country in the world. We had the opportunity to work at a rural teaching hospital for African medical students who had a lack of clinical teachers. In 2011, we returned to the US, joined up with our organization Serge, and after an extensive period of preparation (including a year of French language study), we relocated to Burundi in 2013, where we now live and work.

Both Burundi and our former home in Kenya are in the temperate green and cool of Africa's equatorial highlands. The land and the people are beautiful. Our work in the hospital is beautiful in a different way, but it's also quite restricted. Our medicine supply chains are often interrupted. Our nurses are often overwhelmed by the number of patients they are asked to care for. The hospital goes for long periods without electricity or water, which affects everything from basic visibility (imagine delivering a baby by the light of a mobile phone) to the machines in the operating room to the refrigerator that keeps our blood bank usable. For all that, we are the best game in town and a sign of hope for the people who surround us, and so it is our privilege to continue.

~ ~ ~

Thus ends the strictly biographical part of this book, for biography is not my final goal. Though biography will continue to seep into any story, I primarily want to focus on the heart of the one who goes to serve.

God's transforming grace calls us all to enter into the mess of the world around us. That much is clear. This is often on a personal level, such as a friend going through a divorce or a family member with advanced Alzheimer's disease. It is also often on a vocational level, such as a social worker in a poor community; a counselor hearing a story of past abuse; or as in my case, a doctor in an impoverished corner of Africa. When we seriously try to follow Jesus, we get our hands dirty, and as we confront these needs, they take a toll on our hearts. Sometimes, it hits us all at once. Sometimes, it gradually and cumulatively wears us to the ground. We may be full of doubts, full of helplessness, or full of despair—or we fear we soon will be. It is enough to crush us.

However, in my experience, we don't talk much about the toll these situations exact upon our hearts. When we succeed, we can share our triumphs. When those we're serving struggle, we can discuss their difficulties. After all, that's why we serve. But our own weaknesses? Our own struggles? We assume people don't want to hear about those. Or maybe we don't want other people to view us in that role. We are the helpers, the healers, the servants. We are uncomfortable being the ones who need healing.

Nevertheless, talking about these struggles is unavoidable for at least two reasons. The first reason is the most championed: If our discouragement goes unchecked, we will burn out, or at least emotionally check out. Consequently, the goal of serving others will be hindered either quantitatively or qualitatively by the heart sequelae our efforts have accumulated. The focus is on a task to be accomplished. The would-be servant is a bit like a commodity that should be spent wisely and not foolishly. We are a tool to be used, and in order to be used well, we need to be maintained well. There is some truth in this idea. Overall, this first reason is not so much incorrect as it is insufficient.

The second reason why talking about these struggles is unavoidable is much more overlooked: although we may be tools, we are much more than tools. Paying attention to what is going on in our hearts is much more than routine maintenance on a service vehicle. Indeed, God is completing a task. He is bringing his life-giving kingship to bear on all his broken creation. He will not stop until this is accomplished. Indeed, by his mercy, he brings his children into his work so that we become agents through which his work is done in the world.

We are no different than those we would serve in that we are all sufferers. We are all broken. We are all sinners. We are all in desperate need of God's transforming renewal to resurrect new life inside of us as well as in the world around us. We are not just the catalyst. We are also the substrate. We are called to participate in God's mission, and our very hearts are part of that selfsame seedbed. The kingdom comes through us. The kingdom comes in us. Thus, we need to discuss our sorrows and our discouragements because, as we find new life, new encouragement, and new hope forming in our own hearts, God's truest work is going forth in the world.

So if we are to forge ahead and examine the emotional toll our attempts to help would incur, what do we hope to find? Recognition that such a life is hard is possibly a worthy beginning but not a worthy end. What are we looking for?

The best summary I can offer is this: If we are to walk with those in need and not lose heart, we need to remember the promises of God. This remembrance has two sub-categories: what the promises are and the faithfulness of the one who promises.

~ ~ ~

I want to tell stories from my life and work these last several years. Stories of joy and pain, beauty and tragedy, redemption and lament. In the end, they are mostly stories of trying to find God's light in dark places, both in the world and in my own heart. They are stories of struggling to understand and remember the promises God has given. The storytelling is very intentional because while both theoretical discussions and practical advice have important roles to play, my hope is that the narratives add something else. I hope you can *feel* the tension and identify with it.

Since I received fabulous help in editing them, I unabashedly recommend to you the discussion questions at the end of each chapter. In addition to using them for group study or more rigorous self-reflection, if you get to the end of a chapter and say to yourself, "This is something I should think about more," then consider spending some time with the questions as a way of working that strewn seed a little deeper into the soil of your heart.

My particular circumstances are often stark, but I believe the fundamental constituent pieces of these stories are present in every life, everywhere. I hope the starkness will throw into relief themes that may be cloudier elsewhere, and that this will help these stories to resonate across the particularities of differing circumstances and ring true for your own life, as you seek to walk with those in need.

1

Brother's Keeper

*Like all great commitments, love operates simultaneously
on two different levels: the level of gritty reality
and the level of transcendent magic.*

—DAVID BROOKS[1]

❧

I am supposed to be in Kenya. But I'm not. I'm in Gallup, New
Mexico.

My wife, Rachel, and I finished our medical training a few
months ago. After years of anticipation, we are slated to move
to Kenya for two years to work at a rural hospital. We should
already be there. However, due to a big market slump, our house
won't sell, and so our solution is to get a job for a couple months
and make some money to resolve the issue. Kenya will have to
wait a little longer.

We said "anywhere," and we ended up in Gallup. It is an
interesting place. I don't mean *interesting* as in a more polite
word for *terrible*. Nor do I mean *interesting* as in *always something new going on*. But, it is unique.

Gallup is the high desert with red rock and high winds and snow in the winter. It's Native Americans and old cowboys. It's the classic Route 66, full of wonderfully faded attractions. Gallup is Radiator Springs with a Walmart. And, if you ever pass through on a Saturday morning, it's worth going out of your way on Route 666 (not kidding) to find the Navajo flea market where you can buy grilled mutton, a used tire, a puppy, and tickets to the next ZZ Top concert in Albuquerque—all within a thirty-minute visit.

I am working in an urgent care for the Indian Health Service mostly taking care of Navajo patients while Rachel tries to fill the lonely hours with our five-month-old daughter in a town where we know no one and won't be staying long.

~ ~ ~

The system is understaffed and overwrought. There aren't enough doctors to go around. Despite being an urgent care, we are routinely giving patients return visit appointments to come back and see us here, since it will be months until a spot opens up with a primary care doctor or even longer for specialty services. The staff plod through the long days with an air of routine. They have come here from all over, and who knows why they stayed? Maybe they wanted to help. Maybe they fell in love with the people. Maybe some of them came for two months like me, and now, here they are, seven years later. The patients wait for hours to see me with what seems to be a saintly patience but may just be a truce made of low expectations.

This passivity, which I appreciate when they are waiting on me, has its drawbacks.

"So, your back is hurting you again?"

"Killing me."

"Have you seen your regular doctor about this?"

"Yeah, his office was supposed to call me back at the beginning of September, but they never did."

"September? Almost two months ago?"

"Yeah."

I pause and try to sort out the right thing to say. I haven't been here long, but I've heard this story so many times. The system has its problems, but the patients cripple it further by leaving their part undone.

"Look, I know the system can be frustrating, and communication can be difficult, but this is your health. In the end, you are responsible. You have to call them. Then call them again. I know it would be nice if all the pieces would just fall into place for you, but even when they don't, it's still your responsibility."

He nods and doesn't seem overly put out by my miniature rant. I have a moment's doubt that I said the wrong thing but then decide that continuing to try and address it isn't going to help. I head out of the exam room to fill out some papers for him, and my nurse hands me a form. A patient I saw last week with bad, out-of-control diabetes hasn't shown up for his return visit. It's concerning, since he could certainly get really sick really fast. But he didn't come, so I need to fill out a form saying whether or not I contacted him and what he needs to do.

What does he need to do? He needs to keep his appointment! How can I help him if he doesn't take responsibility? It's his health! If he doesn't care enough about his health, why should I? Am I my brother's keeper?

"Am I my brother's keeper?"[2] Yeah, that's in the Bible. My stance is biblical. Wait. Who said that? Oh yeah. Cain.

Later that night, having a late dinner in our rental apartment, I'm telling Rachel about all this, wanting her to agree that I'm in the right.

"That doesn't sound very compassionate," she intones softly. She reminds me this is not likely to get easier when we move to Africa in a couple months.

I know she's right, but why do people need to make it so difficult for me to help them? Why does the system need to make it so hard for all of us to do what it ostensibly wants us to? And why does my compassion flee at the first roadblock or annoyance? Is it really that thin?

The problems are piling up, and it feels like each little strike is wearing away another layer of my heart. For now, it is raw and exposed. If the erosion continues, maybe my heart will go numb. Paul says to speak the truth in love.[3] Maybe I'm right, but I'm not loving. So apparently that's not enough.

What's going on? There seem to be two issues rolling around inside me—one in my head and one in my heart. I am willing to acknowledge the one in my head—the difficulty of accomplishing a good thing (taking care of a sick person) and the way that a given hindrance (lack of personal responsibility) can make it seem impossible. It's an important issue, and it's worth discussing, if the good thing is worth accomplishing.

The second issue, the one in my heart, is more hidden. In fact, I am probably hiding it from myself on some level. I mean, who wants to acknowledge his own lack of love or compassion? But if I'm willing to look honestly, I find I'm wanting to draw a line, like the man who asks Jesus, "Who is my neighbor?"[4] He wants to know whom he doesn't have to love. I'm wanting to know *when* I can stop loving them.

My friend Bob pointed out once that, in the parable of the Good Samaritan, though the question posed is, "Who is my neighbor?" Jesus's answer is another question, "Which person *was* a neighbor?" Instead of answering the question, Jesus reformulates it. In other words, the question is all wrong because neighborliness is not to be an obligation for his followers. Rather, neighborliness is something Jesus calls his followers to give, to extend, and to offer just as freely as God has offered his grace to us. We choose to become our brother's keeper because Jesus has first chosen to become our brother.

This is my calling, and I know it. The funny thing is that Rachel and I have already structured our lives significantly around a belief that we are called to extend neighborliness. I've never had any kind of lightning-clarity moment where I just knew I was supposed to move to Africa. However, my lack of specific calling in no way negates the importance of the general calling every follower of Jesus has. I did know I was called to steward whatever gifts God gave me for his glory and for the needs of the world he loves. That's why we decided to move to Kenya. And our goal of getting to Kenya is why we are in Gallup.

What does the reaction of my heart reveal? Well, it seems I like this calling more in theory than in practice. I like serving, but not serving this guy. I want to love, but when it comes to loving someone right in front of me, I so often come up short. I know my calling, but I don't want to do it. Thus, this realization is also a calling to repentance.

These truths are essential. They are the heart of the matter, and we must address them. However, they don't automatically make my situation easier. The next day, I return to work, and it's more of the same—inadequate resources, broken lives, overrun systems, harmful choices. Even if I'm acting out of love, how is anything going to improve if I don't have the cooperation of the patients themselves? I'm looking for health, for restoration, for some good thing to come to pass in the lives of these folks. Maybe I can become my brother's keeper, but what am I keeping him for? Where is this going? What are we doing? It seems as if it's all just spinning tires.

~ ~ ~

All these thoughts swirl around in my head as I go from room to room and form to form. I finish work around nine o'clock at night. I zip up my jacket over my scrubs and put my stethoscope in my backpack. Our apartment is about 25 minutes away by foot, so I usually walk to and from the hospital to leave the car free for Rachel. Walking home is nice. It's all downhill, which is just right for leaving work behind you.

The road is empty, and most parts have a sidewalk that's old and cracked, which no one here is ever likely to be bothered by. Under these cold desert stars, with a quiet night street, and the lights of a forgotten town below me, it's easy to let my mind go where it will.

I find myself thinking about eucatastrophes. Maybe this isn't what normal people think about, but I was reading about the idea and trying to wrap my mind around it. It's a literary term, attributed to J. R. R. Tolkien,[5] and (as I understand it) it essentially means victory snatched out of the jaws of defeat. In Tolkien terms, it's all the free peoples of Middle Earth standing before the armies of Mordor and a sure and certain death. It is heroic, and it is tragic. Nevertheless, it is defeat. Then, at the last possible moment, the Ring falls into the fire. In an instant, it is destroyed, and evil crumbles. Out of the deepest defeat explodes a shock of victory. And yet (and this seems to be the distinguishing feature of a eucatastrophe) it happens in a way that makes sense of the rest of the story. It's the best type of ending.

I remember walking out of the theater after the movie version of *The Two Towers*, and a friend of mine, who hadn't read the books, asked me if there was any way good was going to triumph. He couldn't imagine that ending, given the trajectory of the story he had thus far encountered. I had to restrain myself not to give the ending away. My desire to share such a good ending was battling inside me with my desire to not spoil such a good ending for him.

Tolkien said the incarnation of Jesus was the eucatastrophe of history, and the resurrection was the eucatastrophe of the incarnation. In other words, according to Christianity, this is what God does: he makes eucatastrophes. Just like the winter solstice when we celebrate Christmas, it was getting darker and darker until *bam!*—salvation comes. What this means for us now is that, if the stories past inform the stories to come, then Christians have good reason to look for surprising victory.

Maybe it's like that for all of us, toiling in our work and our relationships to see God's kingdom manifest. We are all like masons laying stones on a road. It looks like it's headed out to a desert, with nothing but scrub brush and sand on the horizon. But then, one day, in an instant, we turn the corner of some inconspicuous mesa and find ourselves at the gate of a city—at *the* city. It's where we wanted to go, but where we didn't think we were getting any closer to. Our limited data and our limited perspective would have declared it unlikely, if not impossible, but we were nevertheless on the road all the time. It's a eucatastrophe.

It's what God does. It's a thing of joy and beauty, and the unexpectedness of it all is a testimony that we were led by hands and eyes bigger than our own. And the great grace of it all is that our own small efforts were woven into this mighty arrival. The best type of ending.

~ ~ ~

In the face of all the spinning wheels, in the face of my own utterly unreliable heart, I have two needs. The need in my heart is for vocation: to remember I am called to give love, for such was given to me. I am called to give *unmerited* love, for such is exactly what is still being given to me. The need of my head is for hope: a reason to think all these spinning wheels will one day catch traction at just the right moment, bringing me home at last.

We are called to be our brother's keeper.

We have good reason to look for surprising victory.

If this is all true, then we have both a call and a hope.

And so we go.

QUESTIONS FOR DISCUSSION AND
PERSONAL REFLECTION

1. In what areas of your life do you walk with those in need? In your personal life? In your professional life? What is the sense of calling (if there is one) that brought you to these situations?

2. When such a road gets tough, what thoughts arise in your mind and your heart? What is your gut-level reaction in those moments?

3. When those you are trying to help don't cooperate or when they resist you, how does your heart react? What emotions, thoughts, or feelings tend to rise up in you?

4. Tolkien claims that *eucatastrophe* ("victory snatched from the jaws of defeat") is characteristic of God in the Christian story. Aside from the incarnation and the resurrection, can you identify other biblical examples of eucatastrophe?

5. Is there a story in your own life that could be described as eucatastrophe? Can you imagine that some of your present struggles could be resolved in such a way? What makes it hard for you to imagine this?

2

Insufficiency

*Lord, teach us . . . to find an abundance of your love
in those pockets of our lives where the poverty of our
abilities crowds out our pride and ego.*

—COMMON PRAYER[1]

A couple months later, Rachel and I arrive in Kenya and start working in a large hospital run by a Kenyan church denomination with partnership from many American missionaries. The immediate surroundings are rural, with steep hills covered in small family farms that grow their own food and a bit of tea for a cash crop if they have part of a field to spare. From my American perspective, the hospital services seem incredibly limited, but it's actually quite advanced compared to other care within the surrounding area. The end result is that, despite the remote location, the hospital is booming with incredibly sick patients.

My job will involve working periodically on a variety of hospital services, and I am placed first on the pediatrics service. I don't know who made the decision, but it's a good one. As a family medicine doctor, I don't have a lot of experience caring for really sick kids, and by starting on the pediatrics service, I'll have several months of working with a very experienced pediatrician.

It is a wild ride. Thirty hospitalized kids and thirty more newborns in the NICU. Rushing to deliveries to resuscitate newborns that aren't breathing. Then, the next day, we do it all over again. I am learning a lot and gaining confidence. After three weeks, I'm on call for my first weekend.

~ ~ ~

I'm walking up to the hospital at seven o'clock in the morning. Rachel is holding our baby and gives me a thumbs-up as I head out the door. Down the sidewalk, through the walking gate, up the rutted road, up some stairs, and through the back hospital entrance. I have my day planned out. I'll head straight to the NICU and start seeing newborns. Then, at nine o'clock, I'll go down to the ward, where my intern will have finished seeing the older kids. We'll round. We'll drink some chai. Then, we will return to the NICU and see the rest of the babies. Being home for lunch seems very possible.

My plan lasts for about ten minutes. While seeing my first baby in the NICU, the overnight nurse comes over to talk to me about the two sickest babies. The first is a premature baby who is having difficulty breathing. Okay, this doesn't look good, but we have her on our most aggressive oxygen therapy, and I'm pretty sure we're doing all we can.

The second baby is a full-term baby brought in overnight for severe jaundice. This is worrisome because when a baby gets extremely yellow, he can develop a problem in the brain that acts a lot like bad meningitis. No feeding, rigid body, seizures, coma, death. It's scary and rare. But that's what this baby has. In this case, the problem is due to a lack of that little RhoGAM shot pregnant ladies get routinely in the US if their blood type warrants it. The baby is already under aggressive light therapy, and it doesn't seem we can do any more.

"I was thinking the baby needs an exchange transfusion," says the nurse. Exchange transfusion? I'm familiar with this procedure and its use in a case like this. I've never seen it done, and it hasn't entered my mind that it's something we could do at this hospital. And by *we*, I guess I mean *me*.

Over the next several hours, I contact seven of my doctor friends, pulling each of them out of their well-deserved, restful weekend to give me their input. Two of them actually put on their coats and hike it up to the hospital to help me out. During all this time, the little baby with the difficulty breathing dies.

Several hours later, I get down to the ward, apologizing to the intern for being late. He doesn't mind, since he has been busy trying to take care of a three-year-old with HIV and tuberculosis that we have been trying to save. She has just died. It's noon. No patients have been seen, and two kids have died.

Keep going. Just keep going. Talk with the family whose child has just died. Pray with them. The other children still need to be seen. Keep going.

At eight o'clock at night, I am sitting on a stool in the NICU next to the final incubator, broken clipboard on my lap, writing my final note. The sun has been down for a while, but it is still warm. I'm going to have to get up in the morning and do this all over again.

During the night, they call me up. The jaundiced baby has died. In the morning, another one dies. And then later, during Sunday rounds, another.

Five children die within forty-eight hours.

I won't tell all the stories. To be honest, I don't even remember all the stories. But I do remember that, for each one, when my hand touched their little body for the last time, I would pray to commit this little child into God's hands. And each time, it got a little harder to continue to believe in the subtle and powerful mystery that we proclaim as the goodness of God.

God, why is this happening?

God, no more, please.

God, I believe you are good. Please, show me. I need to see it. These kids. These families. We all need to see it.

There's so much death. How can I keep going?

~ ~ ~

Sunday night, I'm surrounded by friends. They understand, because it's what they do as well. Rachel puts her arms around me and whispers that God's strength is made perfect in weakness. It's the kind of phrase that can only be whispered in a moment of such overwhelming inadequacy.

Tension resides in my heart. It's not a broken faith, but it's tension, like the psalmist and prophets who would rather keep shouting their questions at God than receive an answer from anyone else. God, what do you want from me? You want me to dive into this brokenness? And do what, drown? It's too deep and the storm is too rough. This situation needs someone stronger than me. I thought after all my training that I could do this, but I can't. I don't know how. The needs are just too great.

This is what people do—all of us. To be human is to have moments in life where we come up dramatically short, where we are simply insufficient to the task before us. Since I have become a doctor in rural Africa, these moments have become more frequent and more dramatic. It's always been the case, but now I can't ignore it.

∾ ∾ ∾

When I talk with people about my work, one of the most common responses is to remember the comfort found in knowing I did everything I could do. I agree there is real comfort in that thought. I owe this competency to all of my patients. Wherever we enter into such critical needs, we owe that competency. But what do we do when that also fails?

I remember Mercy.[2] Five months after my first call weekend, I'm less of a novice and starting to find a certain rhythm in hospital life. Visitors now come and ask me where the bathroom is, and I can successfully direct them. The grim realities of the hospital seem a little less piercing, and I'm trying to remember that no one can ask me to do the impossible. I can only do what is possible in my circumstances.

Now I'm taking care of adults in the hospital. Mercy is thirty-five years old. She has at least two little kids. I have seen them around visiting their mom, but odds are good she has more children at home.

Mercy comes in with trouble breathing, and a chest X-ray shows her heart is huge. The hospital staff and I decide she has heart failure and start giving her medicine to get the fluid out of her lungs. But, she just isn't doing well. Something doesn't seem to fit. Then, after a couple weeks of floundering, Mercy's left leg swells up.

That changes everything. If a leg is swollen from a big blood clot, then the trouble breathing is probably due to bits of that clot breaking off and lodging in the lung's blood vessels. Now it seems that, even if Mercy's heart is bad, it isn't the cause of her problem, and our treatment isn't going to help her.

Mercy tells me she had this kind of problem before, a couple years ago. She didn't think it was important enough to tell me when she came in, and I didn't ask.

We hurry to start her on the appropriate treatment. Three days later, she gets up to walk to the bathroom, collapses, and dies. Maybe if we had started treatment sooner for her blood clot, she would have lived. Maybe not. But maybe.

It's hard. She was young. She left at least two little kids motherless. She spoke to me each day in English, and she felt like a sort of friend. Now, Mercy is gone, and maybe if she had a better doctor, if I had been a better doctor, she would still be here.

There is a comfort in knowing you did everything that anyone could have done. This is true. But I am not at all sure that's the case for Mercy and me. I want it to be true, and I tried to make it true. I'm just not sure.

I know God hasn't called me to get it right every time. He has called me to get up again for another day and do the best I can with the gifts he has given me. This also is true, and this also is a comfort. But in the face of all my weakness, sometimes it feels like a pretty small one.

~ ~ ~

Insufficiency is a heavy weight. How can we bear it?

In a letter to a young church, Paul writes about a strange vision where he has a thorn in his flesh and he begs God repeatedly to remove it. God refuses to do so, and then, by way of either justification or comfort, God makes a remarkable statement:

"My grace is sufficient for you, for my power is made perfect in weakness."[3]

For a long time, I thought that statement meant God would find a way to work his will through us *despite* our weaknesses. I thought we could take comfort in our weaknesses from knowing God would not be hindered by them. If this were true, then I would expect Paul's reply to God's words to be, "Okay, but if you take out the thorn, it could be even better!" Paul doesn't say that, because he apparently understood the point better than I.

"My power is made perfect in weakness." It is precisely *in* our weaknesses and not in spite of them that God's power is made perfect. Thus, God decides to leave the thorn, since it is creating weakness and therefore perfecting his power. In my initial interpretation, God is like a manager, helping us along the way, ensuring our weaknesses aren't stopping us from accomplishing something. In the second interpretation, it's God who must act because our weakness shows we can't.

How is God's strength made perfect in weakness? Sometimes I catch a glimpse of it happening, or maybe I could make a guess. However, most of the time, and especially in cases like Mercy's, I honestly don't know. It's a promise, and admittedly we must trust to hold on to it.

There is good reason to trust, however. When Paul said God's power was made perfect in weakness, he was speaking the words of a particular vision but also a truth which he had seen and lived. Paul was often insufficient for the task. He didn't have enough wisdom, enough polished arguments, or enough favor with people. He was beaten, stoned, shipwrecked, and imprisoned. We don't have to read very much of the rest of the Corinthian letters to see the failings of the churches he planted. Paul's entire life was shot through with weakness, but the kingdom of God was going forth nevertheless.

This may seem surprising, but we must at least admit that it bears a certain resemblance to the life of Jesus that the church was trying to follow. From a purely human standpoint, Jesus didn't look like a fortress of strength. His teachings were misunderstood, and his closest disciples so often seemed clueless. Then the powers of the day rose against him and killed him. Through it all, there is weakness. Then God acts. There is resurrection and miracle. Something new comes that could not have come but for the power of God. Thus, Jesus is glorified.

Yet we hold out this tattered world and our tattered attempts to make it better, and we say "God, how can this be the means by which your strength will be made perfect?" It is a consistent biblical phenomenon, yet, it is still a mystery. I don't understand, but I am slowly beginning to think that my lack of understanding is part of the point. Because when I don't know what to do, what happens? I am forced to wait—just wait on God and trust him to do something. The bald fact that I cannot solve or even improve the situation is staring me in the face. It is alternately humbling and humiliating. This is an antidote to my pride, and though I am loathe to admit it, I know my pride is a poison in everything I do—to my family, work, patients, and to my own heart. This antidote has been so elusive, my pride so stubborn and in an unlikely struggle, my pride falters, and new life starts to arrive. Thus we start to suspect that God is once again surprising us.

When God must act because I am weak and cannot act myself, everyone can see that. No one is going to praise me. They will praise God, and this is a good thing. Contrary to what I often feel, the crumbling of my plans is not the crumbling of God's plans. In fact, the crumbling of my shoddy and moth-eaten plans may well be the construction of God's plans, beautiful and strong in the way that I never could have imagined. This was true for Jesus and for Paul and for the birth of the church.

Paul concludes, "Therefore I will boast all the more gladly of my weaknesses, so that the power of Christ may rest on me."[4] Certainly, I can at least admit when I don't know, or when I make a mistake, and this is bound to lead to better care for my patients.

This changes everything for us in our insufficiency. Over the past several years, I have come to believe that we must either be serious about God being glorified in our weakness or we should just stay home because we're not going to bring anything else to the table. We can dress up our skills. We can train for decades. We can try and style the circumstances to capitalize on our strengths. Those aren't bad things, but they don't erase the inescapable truth that we are and will always be insufficient to the task in front of us. The needs around us will always outstrip us. We will always be utterly reliant on the action of God in our relationships, in our work, and in the world. In this we follow the way of Jesus.

So what will we do? We can hide from it. We can pretend it's not the case or, if it is, it's not a big enough deal to change the way we live. Denial is often a default mode. The alternative is we can own our weakness. We can fearlessly and transparently talk about all we cannot do—all the ways in which we are simply relying on God to do something that will, in the end, make all the difference. We can look to him who brings life from the dead and light from the darkness.

God's power made perfect in our weakness. It's truth for us. It's freedom for us. And it's a promise to us.

QUESTIONS FOR DISCUSSION AND PERSONAL REFLECTION

1. When have you felt utterly ill-equipped or weak in being able to care for someone? When you sense your weakness, what narrative does your heart lean toward? What do you try and tell yourself or remind yourself of?

2. Describe a time when you felt called to help someone but were unable to serve them well. How did your heart respond? Where did you go from there?

3. What does it mean to you that God's strength is made perfect in your weakness? How might God do this in a circumstance you're facing?

4. Aside from the examples cited in the chapter, can you think of other biblical examples where God's strength was going forth under the guise of seeming weakness or failure?

5. How does your pride damage your work and relationships? (For extra credit, ask your spouse, family member, or close colleague that question.) How might your weaknesses be the antidote for your pride?

3

Promise

Here and there even in our world,
and now and then, even in ourselves, we catch glimpses
of a New Creation, which, fleeting as those glimpses
are apt to be, give us hope both for this life and
for whatever life may await us later on.

—FREDERICK BUECHNER[1]

❧

In Kenya, chai time is an institution. All across the country, friends gather for a mid-morning pause to enjoy a hot cup of milk, lots of sugar, and just enough black tea leaves to give the drink an off-white color. No one has ever struggled to get me to like a hot beverage, but a sudden mid-morning interruption to our busy hospital work took some adjustment. In the end, I have come to appreciate how chai time gathers our team of Kenyan interns and doctors together to start the next phase of work and often gives us an occasion to laugh. Also, I just really love the chai.

When chai time is done, the cups are emptied, and rounds begin. My team of interns gathers their clipboards, and we head into the male ward. The first patient is breathing seventy times a minute, his lips are blue, and skin is stretched tight over his cheekbones. He has AIDS as well as something bad in his lungs that he could have fought off if his immune system wasn't destroyed by HIV. We don't know what, so we're treating for as many different possibilities as we can. The second patient comes in with a splitting headache. He has HIV as well as a fungal meningitis, so he'll be here for several weeks getting IV therapy. The third patient is in a coma. We don't know a lot about his story, but he looks like a seventy-pound skeleton, and he has violet skin spots all over his chest. He also has HIV.

All in all, about half of the patients on the adult medicine ward have HIV. Many of them have HIV-positive spouses, and some of them have HIV-positive children. They are mostly in their twenties and thirties. They should be out working in shops and on farms. They should be attending the weddings of their distant relatives and singing in the church choir. But they're not. Maybe they won't be ever again. We can treat some of their complications, but it's amazing how hindered medical treatment can be when the body's own immune system doesn't work. Medicines against the HIV itself are available, but the patients have to survive long enough for the meds to kick in, and in the meantime, their bodies are just barely hanging on.

The other half of the ward seems to be full of incurable cancer: stomach, esophagus, liver, whatever. Patients sought treatment too late, and so now the hospital staff and I will do what we can, but curing the cancer is not in that category. Most of them have come a long way, looking for help, hoping we can do something that we just can't do. Bed by bed, person by person, the interns and I make our way around the room, doing what we can and feeling the tremendous weight of all that we can't. It's exhausting. We keep waiting for the good news, but it doesn't seem to come.

However, when we're done, all the family members, who had been patiently waiting outside, come in and crowd the beds. They bring handshakes and news from the village. The kitchen worker rolls her cart down the center aisle, and the family shares a meal of rice and beans and a slice of pineapple. The shift in the room is slight, but it's definite—a little more light. A little of the goodness of everyday human life enters. A bit of consolation sneaks in at the end of a long litany of sorrow. I catch a glimpse of new creation.

～ ～ ～

On another day, a kid comes in to the emergency room malnourished and stiff as a board from meningitis. He's carried by his dad, a gaunt young man with a shabby suit coat and shoes made out of strips of tire rubber. The boy is seven years old. Across Africa, the risk of dying is highest during the newborn period, and it drops progressively throughout the first five years of life. Parents can be somewhat guarded about their hopes for really little kids, but this child is old enough for his parents to believe he's going to grow up to be an adult, go to school, get married, and raise a good crop of maize when the rains come. He should have been out of the danger zone.

I don't know where the child has been for the past week, but showing up already this sick, his prognosis is terrible. When I shine a light in his eyes, his pupils barely constrict. His breathing is irregular. But I never know. I've seen kids like this pull through—now and then. The nurses and I breathe a prayer over him while we get an IV started and give him the best antibiotics we have. An oxygen mask is slipped over his head. We send off some lab tests and try to decide how much fluid he needs. Forty-five minutes later, I have to tell the family he died before we even got him out of the emergency room. Some of them wail. Some of them thank me for what I've done. I don't know which is worse.

But then, as I walk out the door, I see a pair of young brothers, the smaller of the two recovering well from a bad case of pneumonia. They are sitting in a patch of sunlit grass with their mother, happily playing with her red beaded bracelet. Another fleeting glimpse of new creation breaking through the darkness.

~ ~ ~

Life is always like that. I could be walking home after no matter what kind of day, and there would be a gentle breeze, or a frilled frangipani blossom on the sidewalk, or a couple of kids giggling as they run shyly away from me.

Goodness peeks through here and there, now and then. New creation glimmers like a pinprick of light in a black curtain. Even on the worst days, I think I can say that's true. Admittedly, it takes a certain set of eyes to see even that much, but if you're looking, you can find it.

However, Jesus's words loom larger than all these small glimpses—much larger. They would almost be embarrassing if they weren't so utterly lovely. In Revelation, Jesus says, "Behold, I am making all things new."[2] I don't know any other words in the Bible that rend my heart as much as those. It feels like a beauty that's anchored in the very center of the earth, in the very center of the human heart. God has loved us with an everlasting love, and he is making all things new. I'm not sure what we might hope is at the center of the universe, but I don't think it could be any better than that.

But what do we do with this promise? How do we reconcile our world to a promise so bold and so audacious? We are not talking about glimpses anymore—not here and there or now and then, but rather all things new, everywhere. It's not even in the same category. When we talk about "all things," the new creation isn't just the brothers playing in the sun with their mom's beaded bracelet. "All things" is also somehow that other kid, the malnourished one with meningitis who just died. And it's his family, who has to head back home and figure out how to live without him. They have to figure out how to live with the fear that, if this happened to one of their kids, what's keeping it from happening to the others? Where is the new creation in that?

"I am making all things new." How can I honestly stare at the reality all around me and still hold on to something I yearn for with all my being?

~ ~ ~

God gives promises—or maybe one big promise articulated in a thousand ways.

I remember hearing Andrew Peterson sing that, though marriage was harder than he had dreamed, the promises that we make in marriage exist to sustain us in those hard times.[3] The idea is true for all promises. We give promises in order to sustain someone else in a time of need. Of course, the power of a promise ultimately depends on the one who makes it. If I were to promise something impossible, the recipients of that promise would be sustained only to the extent that they were duped. On the other hand, if the God of creation, incarnation, and resurrection—the

God who specializes in eucatastrophes—if *he* promises what seems impossible, well that's another thing entirely.

When I think of Abraham, I picture him with a wondering look on his face, wondering where the fulfillment of the promise is. He's not really doubting, just wondering. He's remembering that day when God said to him, "Go from your country and your kindred and your father's house to the land that I will show you."[4] Abraham goes. Then God gives him promises. You will be a great nation, with descendants like the stars in the sky[5], countless like the sand on the seashore.[6] You will possess all this land. All the nations of the earth will be blessed through you.

Along the way, Abraham has a wild ride. Sometimes he stands tall (like when he selflessly offers the best land to his nephew Lot). Sometimes he falls flat (like when he tries to give away his wife to save his own skin). But God is clearly with him. Abraham becomes rich. Kings seek his favor. Then, when a whole alliance of kings rides off with Lot, Abraham chases them down and conquers them. Yet he's still childless, and he's haunted. Where is this all leading him?

God comes to him and tells him not to fear. His reward will be very great. Abraham's response is telling. "O Lord GOD, what will you give me, for I continue childless?"[7] Believing God's promises isn't easy for Abraham, and that's understandable. He is struggling to reconcile God's promises with his reality. Abraham has lived an incredible life, but the promises are not fulfilled, and unless God changes something, they won't be. Yet God responds with a covenant, another promise. He reiterates that he will do this, and asks Abraham to trust. The tension remains.

The adventures continue. Abraham continues to get it right sometimes and wrong sometimes, and God continues to be with him. Still, Abraham waits. Finally, when Abraham is a hundred years old, his long-promised son, Isaac, is born. A miracle of old age. "God has made laughter for me," says his wife, Sarah.[8] It's the best kind of laughter, a classic eucatastrophe. The promise finally fulfilled. Or is it?

Isaac's birth is incredible, but it isn't stars in the sky. It isn't the sand on the seashore. Isaac is one kid. Arguably, he is not even countable. As for all the land Abraham is to possess, he gets a single field with a cave in it. He buys it to bury his wife and suffers extortion just to acquire it. But Abraham, in his own faulted and imperfect way, clings to the promises of God even so. And then he dies.

What happened? Were the promises false? What would I have thought if I had been Abraham's contemporary and friend? Would I have thought him duped—a man of noble character and admirable tenacity, but at the end of it all, a dead man who labored under two utterly irreconcilable ideas, which were the reality of his life and the promises that God had spoken to him?

Holding on to these promises was not easy, but Abraham did it. The promises sustained him to the end.

Were the promises false? No. We can see that, from our comfortable vantage point of millennia later. His descendants are as countless as the stars in the sky. All the nations of the earth have been blessed through him. The promises were all true but in a way that unimaginably exceeded Abraham's own perspective. Seemingly, God never sought to broaden that perspective, to explain his larger redemptive plans to Abraham so that he would understand. God made a promise and asked Abraham to trust. Like one hand holding on to the earth and one hand grasping the sky, the promise probably felt like it would rip him apart, but it was nevertheless the thing that sustained him.

～ ～ ～

I often feel like I have "here and there" and "now and then" when I'm promised "all things new." I imagine I'm in Abraham's position. I have one son instead of descendants that cannot be counted. I have a little glimpse of the mouth of a cave where I can bury my wife at the end of my life, but I was promised all the land of the nations around me.

There's all this darkness and all this suffering, sometimes injected with little points of golden light. Yes, beauty is found from time to time, but pride and selfish ambition still rule the day. Those who come to me seeking help still die from diseases that are easily curable in other contexts. What's more, odds are good that I will also one day die with the situation of the world still generally the same. So is the promise of new creation false? Does living according to the promise mean living admirably but, ultimately, deceived?

Remember Abraham. He couldn't have foreseen the magnificence of how the promise was fulfilled, but the hope of it sustained him nevertheless. He didn't see it, but he was right. So maybe the same is true for us now, in our point in history. Maybe, for now, all we can see is a big, dark curtain with tiny pinpricks of light shining through. But the smallest pinprick can betray the broadest barrier. There is light back there. It's the sun of day, shining all along, and one day, the curtain will be torn in two.

We live with a promise yet to be fulfilled, and to live with a promise is to live with tension. This tension is not a sign that something is wrong. It simply means we have not yet seen the end of the story. But the mystery is that, precisely in that tension, we find the strength to be sustained.

So we name the promises that the faithful promise maker has given to us, even the ones that make us uncomfortable by their splendor and the ones we just can't comprehend could ever be true.

"Blessed are those who mourn, for they shall be comforted."[9] "The Lord's hand is not shortened, that it cannot save."[10] "He executes justice for the fatherless and the widow."[11] "The God of peace will be with you."[12] "Never will I leave you; never will I forsake you."[13] "Though outwardly we are wasting away, yet inwardly we are being renewed day by day."[14]

I am making all things new.

If the promise was true for Abraham, then maybe it could be true for the boy with meningitis and for his family. Maybe it could be true for every last one of those men and women dying from HIV and cancer, as well as every last one of their friends and family, coming in to share some time and conversation. Maybe it could be true for us as well.

QUESTIONS FOR DISCUSSION AND
PERSONAL REFLECTION

1. What are some biblical promises that have been important to you during your life? What makes these promises meaningful to you?

2. Are there any biblical promises you ignore or minimize in some way because they seem too big to be realistic or to have real-life application?

3. Describe a situation where you have seen a promise of God fulfilled after great difficulty or waiting. How does this past story influence how you approach other difficulties in life?

4. Describe a situation where you have walked with someone in need for whom a particular biblical promise seemed unfulfilled (consider reading Psalm 37:25, Psalm 103:2–6, or Matthew 5:3–7 to remind yourself of the boldness of God's promises).

5. When a promise and your present experience of reality create tension, how can you find trust that God will bring a resolution that you cannot yet see? What makes trust and belief difficult in such circumstances?

4

Despair

*That anyone at all in the world would set
their sad heart and tired hands to the work of wreaking
beauty out of chaos is a monument to Grace.*

—ANDREW PETERSON[1]

❧

He is still quite young, maybe thirty-five years old. He has
the classic sign of Kenyan prosperity—a healthy paunch.
Unfortunately, he also has a bad case of diabetes and an infection
that sent him into overwhelming sepsis. His blood is now full of
unwanted acid, and it's threatening to kill him.

When he shows up in the emergency room, he is slipping in
and out of consciousness. He is forgetting to breathe. His heart
rate is slow. Really slow, like thirty to forty beats a minute, and so
his blood pressure is dropping. The ER staff and I are not really
sure why, but he probably just has a sick heart, in the same way
that everything else is sick.

His wife is there, along with a great cloud of relations. In the
middle of the chaos, she is a picture of strength. She is concerned
but holding herself together. She asks a few questions and watches

everything intently. I'm not sure where her calm comes from. I'm hoping it's not just from trust in our hospital because this guy worries me. When patients come in this sick, their likelihood of going home again is very low, but the staff and I will do what we can.

We transfer him to our little ICU where he's placed on oxygen, antibiotics, and medicines to raise his blood pressure. We give him atropine to raise his heart rate. And it works, for a bit. Then, we give him more. And more. Over the next two days, we empty the hospital of atropine to keep him going. Against the odds, he starts to improve. He wakes up. His blood sugar gets under control. His vital signs stabilize.

With great celebration, we transfer him to the general ward after three days to finish his IV antibiotics and tweak his diabetic medications. I haven't yet seen anyone who was that sick recover as well as he did. Healing like this is the reason I keep going with everyone else. Every once in a while, I get to take care of this guy. His wife is obviously delighted, and I can tell from the way her facial muscles have relaxed into a bit of a smile that her tension has lifted.

Two days later, there is an urgent call. The man in the first bed is in respiratory distress. *The first bed? The man who was in the ICU?*

I run down to see him. He is gasping despite a mask full of free-flowing oxygen. I look him over. His legs are fine. His heart is regular, and air is moving into both sides of his overworked lungs. I have no idea what happened. I run through a mental list of possible interventions, and in this context, none of them seems like a helpful option at all. His wife is standing there, asking me what I am going to do for him. Her face is tightened again with fear, but she is hopeful we will be able to do it all again.

I tell her I can't think of anything else we can do for him. We pray. Within the hour, he dies.

I feel like I'm being mocked because I hoped. Because I thought that, every once in a while, I could beat the odds. What was all that for?

~ ~ ~

Five years later, I am working in Burundi. Alyssa, our team pediatrician, is gone for several months, so I am covering the pediatrics service. The hospital has just opened a little neonatal care room. It's four handmade wooden incubators and three beds for the moms to share. The room is not much, but it can make an amazing difference.

A set of triplets is born, and everyone is talking about them. There is even a bit of fanfare as a local government official comes and presents the mom with a congratulatory gift of several canisters of baby formula (which would be prohibitively expensive otherwise).

The triplets are two boys and a girl. At birth, they each weigh around two pounds. No one gains any weight for at least three weeks, but no one gets really sick either. Then, the triplets hit a slow stride. Each day, I go in and see Mom, and we talk about how much milk to give them. She is quiet but patient. Like a typical village woman, she is wrapped in a colorful drape of red fabric. Her hair is styled with the half-inch cut of a villager. Whenever I tell her how I want to change one of her baby's feeding regimens, she turns her head to one side, considering what I just told her. After taking a few moments to think it out, she (usually) assents in a quiet voice.

Months pass. Every day seems the same. The babies take the tiniest steps toward progress. After about three months, we all celebrate. The oldest and largest of the triplets has reached the minimum weight to go home. He is discharged from the hospital, though he will, of course, have to wait with his mom until his siblings reach the same milestone. His mom has given him the name *Dieudonné*, which means *God-given*.

The next day, I am told Dieudonné had a fever overnight, and now Mom says he's not breastfeeding well. I look him over. He seems fine, but I'm not taking any chances. We admit him back into the hospital and start him on aggressive antibiotics.

Around ten o'clock that night, he dies.

I can't believe it. After months of endurance and a marathon victory, all the progress is swatted away in a moment. I don't feel guilty. Just sad and defeated.

The next morning, I go and find Mom at the cistern washing her clothes. Someone indicates to her that I am looking for her. She walks over to me, soap suds still on her hands, her head turned to one side as if she is contemplating some new feeding regimen. This time she can't seem to decide where to look.

In halting Kirundi, I give her my condolences. Tears well up in her eyes. She tells me she's afraid her other son is sick now. For the first time, she says she just wants to go home. She's not being defiant. She's despairing.

These circumstances remind me of the diabetic Kenyan man. They feel like a mockery. Even his name, *Dieudonné, God-given*, feels like a mockery now that he's been taken away. How can I work and work and work until I start to hope for that which I was afraid to hope for in the beginning, and then, in a moment, everything's gone? It's gone in a way that seems to taunt me and ask, "You really thought this was going to happen?"

How can we bear up under such despair? How can we continue to try and hope when the next person comes our way? The walls are too tall. The sun is too dim. The silence is too loud. The pit is too deep and too dry. It's just too much.

~ ~ ~

The breadth of human experience that is articulated in the Bible repeatedly amazes me. I have come to believe there is no emotion that cannot find its echo somewhere in those pages.

> All the day my enemies taunt me;
> those who deride me use my name for a curse.
> For I eat ashes like bread
> and mingle tears with my drink,
> because of your indignation and anger;
> for you have taken me up and thrown me down.
> My days are like an evening shadow;
> I wither away like grass. (Psalm 102:8–11)

Against all my expectations, God has given me words to voice what I am feeling. Though this psalm is not a solution, it's of great value.

> "All the day my enemies taunt me. . . . You have taken me
> up and thrown me down."

I am permitted to voice this frustration. Given that the Psalter is the source book for the corporate worship of the people of God, I am actually commanded to do so. I can read these words. I can write my own. Or, in the moments when my distress is more of an inarticulable groan, I can simply hold these things before God and simply groan, "Look at this!"

The Psalms are rife with such language, but not just the Psalms. Job cries out. The prophets cry out. Even Jesus cries out. These are the sections of the Bible we usually gloss over, feeling vaguely uncomfortable. The culture of Christianity I grew up in has little place for these kinds of brazen emotions, so sermons tend to be preached on other topics—anything else, really. Avoidance works for a time, until believers find they identify with these often overlooked verses. And then we cling to these impassioned words like a strange lifeblood, though, at first, we may not be sure we can trust them.

The Bible calls it *lament*. I called it *despair*. Is it the same thing? Michael Card claims the two are polar opposites. He says that "lament is the deepest, most costly demonstration of belief in God. Despair is the ultimate manifestation of the total denial that He exists."[2]

I picture these moments of desperation as though I'm standing on the edge of a cliff, and only darkness unfolds before me. There is a chasm to cross, but it seems hopeless. Lament, in this image, is like a rope. It may seem pointless to cast out this rope into the darkness, but we are told to cast it out even so. Then, against all hope, I feel the other end of the rope which is still in my hand go taut. Somewhere, out in the darkness, the rope has caught on something. It pulls tight, making a connection between me and the other side. Thus, lament becomes a mysterious bridge that carries me slowly across the seemingly impassable chasm to a place of healing and trust. Lament's opposite, despair, just stares at the chasm that cannot be crossed and the rope that is futile to throw. When this is where we are, how do we move from despair to lament?

There is no simple answer, but I have come to agree with Card that the crux of the matter is not so much *what* I am saying but *to whom* my complaint is addressed. In lamenting, believers can complain about almost anything, but they direct their complaint to God. Job can even say, "I cry to you for help and you do not answer me; I stand, and you only look at me."[3] Notice how Job says *you* and not *him*. On the other hand, as Card says, if despair is a denial that God exists, then despair may complain about God, but it will not cry out to God. No matter what the complaint, no matter what the state of my heart, I will do better to address it to God than to lay it before anyone else. This is what I think makes the difference between despair and lament.

I can feel the difference it makes sometimes. When there is anguish in my heart and I cry out to God, regardless of what I cry, it feels less like despair. Lament takes time, of course, and it is likely to leave scars. What remains is not joy, and it might not even be hope. But there might be a little hope shining through somewhere. In the complicated way typical of real life, lament is not a tour de force, but the shift in my heart is real—just enough to help me trust in the promise that lament offers.

In the end, the permission to lament as well as the storehouse of preserved biblical laments are gifts to us. Lament is a means of grace to us in some of our most desperate times. Lament offers the freedom to come as we are and bare our hearts. Lament offers the comfort that our crushed hearts do not repel God, but rather that "the LORD is near to the brokenhearted and saves the crushed in spirit"[4] We can even pray "The Lord has become like an enemy"[5] or "O LORD, why do you cast my soul away?"[6] or "Why do you forget our affliction and oppression?"[7] Whatever the state of our hearts, the Bible has been there before us. These are the words of Scripture in the mouth of one who is brokenhearted. The Lord is near to such as these.

Lament implies a promise as well. First of all, laments are dynamic. Almost all of the psalms of lament demonstrate clearly that where the psalmist begins is not where the psalmist ends. Lament puts us on a journey, and the fact that it's a journey promises the darkness will not endure forever. And the fact that God sets us out on the path and bothers to send daily bread in the form of words of lament means he thinks the journey worthwhile.

Second, lament also speaks of the promise of God's faithful presence. He is not afraid of our anger or our disappointments, regardless of whether those feelings stem from our circumstances or even with God himself. All of which suggests that, though his presence may be shrouded, we have reason to be confident that he's still with us.

~ ~ ~

At the end of 1 Corinthians, Paul tells of a mystery, which is also a promise.

> Then shall come to pass the saying that is written:
> "Death is swallowed up in victory."
> "O death, where is your victory?
> O death, where is your sting?"[8]

Death is many things, and mockery is one of them. It crashes down into our hardest efforts to give light and life in this world with the smirking ease of a spoiled bully.

The promise is that, at the end of it all, death will be mocked. Death will be taunted.

Now, that will be something.

QUESTIONS FOR DISCUSSION AND PERSONAL REFLECTION

1. What does this chapter suggest is the primary promise God offers us in our despair? Do you agree, or do you have another way to articulate what God promises?

2. Describe a time when your efforts to care for someone threatened to cause despair. What made this particular situation so hard? If your despair had words, what would have been its script?

3. How do you relate to the passages of lament in the Bible? Does this way of talking with God feel familiar or foreign to you? Describe a passage of lament in the Bible that has made you uncomfortable.

4. What are the places in your relationship with God where you'd like to have more freedom to express your heart to him? What causes you to hesitate?

5. How do lament and despair look different in your own life? What is the difference in their impact on the state of your heart?

6. When you recognize despair in someone else, what could you do/say to shift that person toward lament instead of despair?

5

Hope

Hope does not disappoint us.
—ROMANS 5:5 (RSV)

Hope deferred makes the heart sick.
—PROVERBS 13:12

❧

I say goodbye to my kids and head up to the hospital. It's only about a five-minute walk, slightly uphill. The morning air in Burundi is almost always cool, and my hands are in the pockets of my white coat. I'm staring at the red dirt road as I walk, so as to not to trip over the uneven ground. The primary school is on my right. One of the teachers is banging a traditional cowhide drum with a wooden baton. The drum is big, basically a hollowed-out tree trunk, and the cowhide is fastened to the top using rough wooden pegs. He is beating it to call the children to class for the day, and the beat resounds through the hills. For a moment I'm caught up in a wave of children running to the school entrance. As some of them shyly avoid me, others go out of their way to shake my hand and greet me in English.

"Good morning! How are you?"

"I'm fine, thanks," I say. "And how are you?"

"Fine, thank you. And you?"

"Uh, fine . . . "

"Fine, thank you," they say. "And you?"

I can see where this is going (or not going), so I just smile and keep walking. Beyond the wave of children, my thoughts turn to the day. Alyssa, the pediatrician, is gone for the day, so after seeing the adults on the internal medicine service, I'm going to go over and see as many of the children as I can. It's more work, but I'm looking forward to the variety.

As it turns out, I don't have many adults to see, and I make it over to pediatrics by midmorning. Since I'm not sure I'll be able to see all of the children, I ask the nurse to take me first to those who need the most attention. She takes me straight to Emmanuel.

Emmanuel is ten years old, and he's been in the hospital for a couple weeks. I've heard Alyssa talk about him. He came with persistent fever and confusion. In Burundi, the two most common causes for that combination of problems are severe malaria and bacterial meningitis. This boy was tested for those two things. The tests didn't show anything, but the tests aren't perfect. Emmanuel is really sick, so we are treating him anyway. Nevertheless, he's not getting better.

Then, last night, his nose started bleeding—a lot. Despite our best efforts, it's still bleeding. Blood is on the bed and on his shirt. A small pile of blood-soaked scraps of cloth lies on the floor next to his bed. For the moment, Emmanuel is laying still with his eyes closed. But his mother looks beyond exasperated. She has already spent a couple weeks of caring for her intermittently confused and agitated son. Now, she has passed the night caring for his profusely bloody nose.

I am pretty sure I know what's going on because I've seen it many times before. I order a complete blood count, and a little later, when the results are back, I gather the medical students together to discuss the situation.

Everything is low. His platelets are low, which is why his nose won't stop bleeding. He is severely anemic, even more than his blood loss would account for. His white blood cells are low, which makes him incredibly susceptible to any kind of infection. This condition usually happens when the body's bone marrow fails to produce the necessary parts of the blood.

The students have questions. What causes it? Lots of things: chemicals, medicines, infections to name a few. Can we figure out what caused it for Emmanuel? No, not here. The tests that could show the cause aren't that complicated, but they are not available here or anywhere else where Emmanuel could receive care. Can we treat the problem even though we don't know the cause? No. Can we just give him a big blood transfusion and call it good? Sadly, no. That won't help his platelet problem, and since that's the source of his bleeding, his blood level will fall again rapidly. Then what are we going to do? Not much. But we will do what we can.

~ ~ ~

Every night, as part of the bedtime litany, my daughter Maggie and my son Ben pray for sick people.

That night, with the two of them lying in bed, Maggie says, "I want to pray for that boy at the hospital who might not get better." Apparently, she had been listening during dinner to my discussion with Rachel about this boy.

"What's his name?" Maggie asks.

"Emmanuel," I say.

Fresh off last year's advent curriculum, Maggie gets excited. "Emmanuel! That means 'God with us!'"

I'm torn. It's hard to pray for him. My technical mind knows his prognosis is grim. I've seen many of these cases, and when people here are as sick as Emmanuel, recovery is unlikely. I can pray for his healing, but what are his odds of survival when he is actively hemorrhaging, even now in his hospital bed just a few minutes walk away, despite all our efforts to make it stop? I am hesitant to hope, probably because that requires risking a part of my own heart, and I'm afraid it won't be worth the risk.

And what am I going to tell my daughter if she asks later what happened to him, and the truth is he's now gone to be with God? That he will never again run through the groves of banana trees, on his own red dirt path, watching his feet so as not to trip on the uneven ground?

I believe these are important discussions to have, but I'm not sure it's a conversation I want to have with my four-year-old. If I'm hesitant to hope for my own heart, I'm even more so for my young daughter's heart.

But she is in earnest, and I don't want to have to explain why I *don't* want to pray for him. So we pray for Emmanuel. The following night, it's the same thing. Night after night, she asks to pray for "the boy whose name means 'God with us.'" We continue to pray, and I continue to feel torn.

After a few days, Alyssa tells me that the bleeding has stopped. A few more days and his fever goes down, and his agitation and confusion lessen. Then, one day, Alyssa walks into the room, and he is sitting up and shakes her hand. Hope stirs. Yet, I remain guarded. I can remember too many other cases. I remember the diabetic man in Kenya.

A few hours later there is an urgent call. He has fallen into a coma. Hope falters. Is this going to be another case of despair? Another case of just enough progress for hopes to be dashed? The story quickly surfaces that his mother has had no money to buy any food for Emmanuel or herself for the past three days. Some food is immediately found and, with a few calories in his system, he wakes up again.

Two days later, Emmanuel is discharged from the hospital in a normal state of mind with no bleeding and no fevers. I don't know where he is now. Emmanuel went home with a very serious condition, one that could easily relapse. It's possible he got sick again. It's also possible Emmanuel recovered, his bone marrow slowly woke up, and now he is back to his old self. Maybe he's back at school, part of the big crowd of happy faces gathered in a courtyard around a great wooden drum.

∼ ∼ ∼

I do have hope that this is the case. For me, hope was unexpected in Emmanuel's case. Sometimes, we can think of hope as something we need to generate. We might tell ourselves if we can just force our minds into a certain hopeful train of thought, then hope will be victorious. And that works—until it doesn't.

Paul writes that "hope does not disappoint us."[1] Proverbs says that "hope deferred makes the heart sick."[2] Once again, I am impressed with this ancient book's appreciation for life's complexity. Hope also holds a promise. But holding on to it is risky.

I wanted to hope, but I was afraid to hope. It was kindled nonetheless. So hope was more a gift than a choice. Maybe that's how hope works.

"'Behold, the virgin shall conceive and bear a son and they shall call his name Immanuel' (which means, God with us)."[3]

Emmanuel. God with us. This is the story of the incarnation and a world that was afraid to hope. The world had borne too much tragedy too many times to hope again. The world wasn't even looking for it anymore. And yet, hope came.

When the disciples huddled together behind locked doors for fear of the Jewish leaders after the crucifixion of Jesus, they were not looking for hope.[4] Maybe they thought they were done with hope. Their dashed hopes had made their hearts sick, and they weren't going to do that again. But then, in a moment, as a gift, God was with them.

In just such a way, hope is less something we need to generate than it is a gift we receive. Yet in another sense, we also need to learn hope. We need even to teach hope to one another. Maybe, as God gives hope as a gift to us, we can learn to give it as a gift to each other. This is not mere optimism, but we can build hope on the foundation of God, the faithful promise maker and the weaver of eucatastrophes. As a doctor, my problem-solving nature will dwell on the cases that are not being fixed. I will spend 90 percent of my time on the 10 percent of my patients who are the sickest. Though this is fitting in a way, it does not necessarily teach hope. How do we give the problems we face due attention without feeling shrouded over by the darkness?

During my daily rounds through the hospital, I do better to take a little time to intentionally remember my reasons for hope. Before moving on from the malnourished girl who's now doing well or the formerly comatose boy with malaria who's likely to go home tomorrow, I can draw my team's attention to these people, who have little left to teach us in terms of medicine but have much to teach us in terms of hope. Let's take a moment to remember. Let's draw attention to the reason for our hope.

These precious people could have so easily died. But they didn't. They are well. The virgin *did* bear a child. The grave did *not* hold him down. God *did* hear the prayers of a trusting child and her hesitant father. And Emmanuel did go home.

Hope is kindled. Maybe the surprise of it all will be enough to teach me to hope a little more.

QUESTIONS FOR DISCUSSION AND
PERSONAL REFLECTION

1. What does this chapter suggest is the primary promise that
    God offers us when we are afraid to hope? Do you agree, or
    do you have another way to articulate what God promises?
2. Describe a time when you have been afraid to hope. What
    was the most difficult aspect of that situation? Why were you
    afraid to hope?
3. Describe a time when your hopes were greatly surpassed and
    you were surprised. How does this experience inform your
    fears about present or future challenges? How does it impact
    your posture as you come alongside those who are hurting?
4. Trusting that God is present, powerful, and loving in our
    world and in our lives is at the heart of the Bible's mandate
    for God's people. Stories from our own lives support this.
    Why is it still so difficult for us to trust and to find hope?
    What gets in the way? When it's not easy to trust, what might
    you be failing to believe?
5. What habits or practices can help us to foster hope, both in
    ourselves, and in those around us?

6

Time

Every day you have less reason not to give yourself away.
—WENDELL BERRY[1]

About five weeks after delivering her baby, Claudette's legs start swelling—a lot. Then her vision becomes blurry, so she comes to the hospital. There we find her blood pressure is sky-high—high enough to be damaging her vision and probably her heart. We run a test to see how her kidneys are functioning, and discover that they basically aren't. Really, it's shocking she is still alive with so little kidney function.

We admit Claudette to the hospital and start treating her blood pressure, hoping that this whole problem is an unusually late complication of her recent pregnancy that will be resolving, or at least relenting, soon. With the medicines she receives, her vision starts to improve, and the swelling in her legs goes down significantly. We prescribe her some blood pressure pills that she will need to take at home. We set up a date for a follow-up visit in two weeks and discharge her home.

But Claudette doesn't go home. The next day, she remains in the same bed and the day after that as well. Her six-week old baby stays with her this whole time, which is not unusual in Burundian culture. What is unusual is that the baby is her only companion. She has no one to cook her food, no one to help her get around, and no one to buy her penny-a-day blood pressure pills from the pharmacy. She just waits. No one comes to take her home. Where is her husband? Her mother? Are they off searching for money to pay for her hospital stay, or have they abandoned her?

About five days later, Claudette tanks. Though she has remained at the hospital waiting for her family to take her home, she hasn't been treated since her discharge. Her blood pressure soars again, and the leg swelling increases. This time, fluid is also collecting around her lungs, and she is having a terrible time breathing. She says her chest hurts. She is leaning forward in her bed, eyes wide, each breath a gulping struggle. The hospital staff rolls in an old bedside oxygen concentrator and she puts on the nasal tubing.

Claudette's prognosis is grim. With no signs that this problem is abating as she gets further out from her pregnancy, and with nearly non-functioning kidneys (a condition that's unlikely to significantly improve), there's less and less we can do. Dialysis could save her, but there are twelve dialysis beds in the country, and none anywhere nearby. Claudette doesn't have pennies for her medicines, much less hundreds of dollars for a single dialysis session. Like always though, the hospital staff and I will do what we can.

Against expectations, Claudette pulls through the crisis. She gets off oxygen and is breathing fairly well. Her blood pressure isn't perfect, but it improves. Her baby remains healthy, managing not to catch any of the numerous contagious diseases present in the other beds of the poorly ventilated room where she stays.

Claudette is quiet. She knows she is sick—very sick. Her aloneness is conspicuous. We have no hospital cafeteria. Her family is supposed to provide her with food. This, of course, means she wasn't eating. The other families in the room with her have noticed this and, out of their own poverty, they are sharing their own food with her.

A week later, and she is ready to be discharged again. She is still alone, so I surreptitiously go and buy her pills for her, in hopes of avoiding a repeat of last time. She continues to wait. For whom? Does she even know?

On the day of her third admission (due to recurrence of the fluid around her lungs), her sister shows up. She wants to take her home—today. Claudette wants the same. I can't blame her, but now is not the moment. I know her prognosis is poor, and I want her to go home too. However, I explain that, if we can just treat her for another day or two, I think that she will be able to go home for a longer period of time. After a big discussion, her sister is reticent, and Claudette passively looks at her swollen legs. They agree.

～ ～ ～

We're buying time. In a very real sense, this is what we're always doing. It's the reality of medicine in a mortal world. No one's physical life is saved forever. Even for a young, healthy person with a reversible disease, we are still buying time, just more of it, so the decision goes without saying.

Claudette needed dialysis weeks ago, but she won't get it. She needs a kidney transplant. She needs an ICU with intensive monitoring of her blood pressure and her electrolytes, but she won't get those things either. But she has gotten some time.

Why bother? Tragic as it all is, what is the good of a few more weeks, at most a couple months? Buying time is just staving off the inevitable. That's true. But think about this time. Each day is another day to know her baby. Each day is a day for her baby boy to grow a bit stronger and increase his tenuous chances of being okay after his mom is gone. Each day is a day to receive a beautifully sacrificial gift of food from the families of her fellow sufferers.

She does go home, after a couple more days. I never see her again, and I doubt that's because she's healthy. But I can imagine her at her home—mud walls with cracked whitewash. The roof is covered in red clay, half-pipe ceiling tiles. Claudette is sitting in the doorway with her baby on her lap, maybe watching another sun come up and listening to the wind rustle the eucalyptus leaves. This is time worth buying.

≈ ≈ ≈

However, the value of this time is more than that, even. Within the time we have, we do. We create. But who knows what might be done in us, what might be created in us? People speak of "buying time" because then they can spend it. This is true: time is opportunity. It's potential. More time isn't necessarily better in and of itself, but there's an opportunity to fill time with something of value.

Yet, as rich as that is, if we leave it at that, I think we are underestimating time. God gave us a world in which time is not just bought and spent like a simple commodity, but time also passes. This quality is so obvious it's usually overlooked. The foundations of creation are embedded in an already-given time. In Proverbs, wisdom is described as the first of God's creative works, a "master workman" for all the subsequent creative acts of God.[2] Time has a similar foundational character. God placed all of his creation *in time*. Time was before everything, and it continues to be a master tool for the mysterious working of God's will.

Wind blows on the mountains. Rivers run in the valleys. And nothing much happens. But in the passage of time, the mountains are worn and the canyons are carved. Also, with us, there's so much that only time can do. Grief cannot be hurried, and neither can friendship. We need time to pass. When we say, "It feels like I've known him for a long time," we testify that time is the rule for the richness of relationship. Time will heal. Time will work on us. Time will shape us with a precision that cannot otherwise be found.

This is another reason why time is so worth buying. Time gives us an opportunity to exert our own wills, yes. But who knows what else may happen in the passage of time?

⮜ ⮜ ⮜

All of this is a call to patience, which is something I badly need. Often, I am covered with impatience, and it doesn't even feel like impatience to me. Impatience rarely does. I'm not impatient; progress is just too slow.

Some days, there's just so much that's broken in the world. We run out of medicines for patients like Claudette. We need to find a way to feed our hungry patients. The oxygen concentrator is broken again. Our medical students have an unexpected absence. The generator is not built for the level of strain we're putting on it. Electricity is out again, and now the faucets are dry.

Bigger problems exist too—much bigger. Problems of public health, national security, and economic development loom. That list goes on and on. These problems seem so overwhelming that we don't even think to tackle them. But the everyday, local problems seem so fixable. We can install a new oxygen system or improve our inventory process so medicines don't run out of stock. These things aren't easy, but comparatively, these are the low-hanging fruits, ready to be picked. These things ought to be controllable. But we still can't seem to get them done. An unforeseen snag occurs somewhere, blocking the way forward. Or someone has a vague resistance to the solution, which might be for a very good reason, but it makes no sense to me. So, every day, it's tripping and crawling. Rising, planning, implementing, then more tripping and more crawling. I want it fixed.

I don't shout in my impatience. When another obstacle comes my way in the hospital, I usually stop talking, and I look off to the side with my hand rubbing my eyes. After a few seconds of silence, with my medical students' gazes on me, I struggle to bring the conversation beyond the disappointment back to the task at hand, whatever the limitations. But these things build up inside me, and I have less patience with each cumulative problem. It spills over eventually, usually with me scolding one of my kids unreasonably for some small infraction.

The great, underlying assumption of my impatience is that I have a firm grasp of the necessary timing for when all these things ought to come to pass. I automatically assume my perspective gives me an understanding of when this needs to be done, and the answer is almost always, "Now."

In this, I am underestimating time, as well as the one who holds time in his hand. The Old Testament is full of people crying out, "How long?" The psalmist says, "It is time for the LORD to act, for your law has been broken."[3] And as far as I can tell, the Lord did not then act, at least not in the way the psalmist had decided was necessary.

We are invited by these words to join in crying out, "How long?"—but there is something else to remember. The story of Abraham is a great example of how God's timing is *bigger* than our own. In addition, Paul writes that God sent forth his son "when the fullness of time had come."[4] Emmanuel came when all the threads in God's mind-bogglingly complex tapestry were most suited to receive him. To put it another way, God's timing was also *better* than our own.

~ ~ ~

Wendell Berry, the old farmer poet, walks up the hill behind his Kentucky home—not too far but far enough to turn around and see everything: his garden, the barn, the pasture. Spring has come, and the branches have filled in with young green buds and replaced the starkness of March. He ends his reflections with these lines:

> Birdsong had returned
> to the branches:
> the stream sang
> in the fold of the hill.
> In its time and its patience

beauty had come upon us,
greater than I had imagined.[5]

"In its time and its patience." It is a striking combination. "Its time" suggests a timing that does not belong to mankind, one that is paired with a patience that's also beyond our own. Berry is surprised by the beauty of it all. It wouldn't be so beautiful without the passage of time. It wouldn't be so beautiful if we had forced it according to our own timing.

～ ～ ～

And so, a call to patience is a call to trust. To trust that, in time, God will do more than we could do in our own timing. This trust is not easy. It is not automatic. After all, with lots of time, maybe everything will just disintegrate. But learning to trust means learning to let God's timing direct, to not obsess when things don't go according to our own timing. Rather, we trust in the possibility that something better is happening, even though we can't see it.

All this sounds so appealing as a concept, and yet I vehemently resist as soon as it's put into practice. Why do we insist that our own limited perspective and timing must be better than whatever God could be doing? Do we even have any confidence that he is, in fact, doing anything? Do we find ourselves curious about what story he's weaving, and if not, what does that say about us?

The good news is, of course, that God calls us to patience because he himself is patient with us. The invitation still stands. It pierces through our resistance, and there remains both a light and a lightness that comes from living in the trust that a timing

greater than our own and a patience greater than our own are
ultimately at work.

Thus again, even in time itself, I find a reason to hope: Hope
for those whose time is so limited and so precious; hope for a
time when all the stray threads and frustrated efforts will be
woven together by a timing better than my own; hope that one
day I too will look down the hill, all strewn with pine and banana
trees, all the way down to the clearing where the hospital hides,
and say,

In its time and its patience
beauty had come upon us,
greater than I had imagined.

QUESTIONS FOR DISCUSSION AND PERSONAL REFLECTION

1. What does this chapter suggest is the primary promise God offers us when we are impatient? Do you agree, or do you have another way to articulate what God promises?

2. Describe a time when your patience has been utterly overwhelmed. What was the hardest aspect of that situation? In the midst of that, how easy or hard was it to consider the possibility of a bigger story that God was weaving? What made it easy or hard?

3. How does impatience manifest itself in you? Do you become angry, cold, sarcastic, or some other reaction?

4. Remembering that God has placed his creation in the flow of time, what are some things in people that can only happen with the passage of time?

5. Describe a time when you recognized that God's timing was better than your own. What happened as a result?

6. Describe a time when you think God's timing was doing something bigger than what you had planned. What was the result?

7

Ordinary

This ordinary time is
gifted in its quiet, marked passing
Christ slips about
calling and baptizing,
sending and affirming,
pouring his Spirit like water
into broken cisterns,
sealing cracks and filtering our senses,
that we may savor the foolish
simplicity of his grace.

—"PASSING ORDINARY TIME" BY ENUMA OKORO[1]

᠊᠊᠊

Most days are just another day. Since Burundi is near the equator, the sun always rises between six and six thirty a.m., and our family rises around the same time. Rachel and I wake the kids and find something for breakfast. To try and simplify an already complicated grocery situation, we have a lot of meal schedules. Monday breakfast is a local multi-grain porridge called *busoma*. On other days, we eat eggs, oatmeal, yogurt, or more *busoma*, depending on the day. Saturday is always pancakes.

Sunday is corn flakes that we buy in a big box from a grocer in the city, then back to *busoma* on Monday. Water for cooking and for our pot of coffee comes from the filter bucket, so hopefully we didn't leave it empty last night.

After breakfast, we get the kids dressed and everyone brushes their teeth. The electricity is almost never on overnight, and thus hot water in the mornings is a rarity. Given that it's always chilly in the morning, Rachel and I usually wait and try to fit in a shower whenever the water supply, electricity, and a few minutes of free time all align. When everything is done, I throw on my white coat and head out the door.

I walk about five minutes to the back hospital gate. I greet random passersby along the road and then hospital staff as I enter the gate. At seven thirty a.m., a brief chapel service takes place for all the staff. We sit on backless benches and sing a song in Kirundi, then someone stands up and gives a brief exhortation. We pray and then announcements for the day are delivered.

Students disperse to their various services to start seeing their patients, and I pass by the emergency room to see if anyone needs urgent attention. If not, I retire to a small office to pray and read the Bible until rounds start. The cloud of students is usually waiting for me when I show up, sitting on call-room mattresses and chatting with one another, laughing. Or they're bent over a final patient chart, finishing up their notes for the day. We pray for healing and wisdom and then start seeing our patients.

The patients are a mixed bag. We start in the isolation building. The first guy has HIV and tuberculosis and seems to be slowly getting better. He's been here a long time and would be ready to go home, but every time we broach the subject, he brings up a new problem. He's always alone, and I don't know if that has anything to do with it.

The second guy has tuberculosis but not HIV, and he seems in good spirits. The bed across from him is a guy with malaria who came in with blood in his urine. He's getting better, even though we gave him the same exact treatment as the hospital that referred him to us. The last patient in isolation is an elderly woman who came in with dysentery. She's doing fine with appropriate antibiotics, so she can go home today. It's nice to see such a straightforward recovery.

In the main wards, the mix goes on. Some patients are getting better. Others aren't. Some have a very clear problem, and we can treat it. Some of them have a clear problem that we can't treat. Others are mysteries that are very unlikely to be solved in light of our limited diagnostic tools. Some are weathering the storm. Others are struggling to keep fear and despair from overwhelming them.

At each bedside, the student gives me the report of the patient overnight, and we talk about how the patient is doing. The students have a lot of questions, and most of them show a curiosity and initiative that will serve them and their future patients well. Other students are passive and distracted, which makes them a challenge to engage. But for every patient, the final question is always the same: "What can we do to help them?" Sometimes it's clear. Other times, it feels like a shot in the dark. Nevertheless, we decide and move on.

We usually finish in time for a late lunch, so I walk home and eat whatever was left over from the kids' lunch. I write a few emails and talk with Rachel and the kids. The afternoons hold more variety. Maybe I will hang out in the ER. Maybe I will have a meeting or deliver a lecture to the students.

When the work day is done, I come home and trade my white coat for a hooded sweatshirt since the day is rapidly cooling off. My favorite evenings are when all the kids on the team are running around outside together and their parents are sitting on a porch talking. Sunset is as prompt as sunrise, usually during the middle of dinner, and then the kids get ready for bed. When they are done, Rachel and I discuss our four after-bedtime activity options: watch a movie, play a game, read books, or continue to work.

~ ~ ~

It's all so ordinary, and this takes a lot of people by surprise. When they come to visit, everything is different, and nothing is automatic. They don't know where to get drinking water or how to use a mosquito net. They aren't sure how they'll cope with cooking everything from scratch or long power outages. It seems difficult (and it can be) and exotic (which it rapidly ceases to be). Before I moved to Africa, all of my travels had this stimulating energy to them. I felt alive and everything was so interesting, so different. I was on the opposite side of the world, seeing things that so few people I knew had seen.

When I actually moved to Africa, that sense of energy dissipated almost instantly. Because now America was on the other side of the world. I was just *here*. And everyone around me had been *here* their whole life. It's ordinary.

Even the medical care, with all of its highs and lows, becomes ordinary. It's normal to have dramatic circumstances. Visiting doctors find that hard to believe, but within a few weeks, they are accustomed to things that had shaken them when they first arrived.

Some of these amazingly difficult decisions, the unlooked-for victories, and the crushing tragedies leave an indelible mark on me. I can remember all the details of those stories. But most of them get all mixed up together into a great big multitude, which, in turn, defines a new normal.

Life is ordinary, and that can be a very good thing.

Ordinary means rhythm and familiarity. Ordinary is a favorite song that has been played a thousand times or homemade pizza every Friday night. Ecclesiastes says, "There is nothing better for a person than that he should eat and drink and find enjoyment in his toil."[2] Proverbs calls it a blessing to "rejoice in the wife of your youth."[3] Zechariah describes God's presence and the result of Israel's purification with the simple image that "every one of you will invite his neighbor to come under his vine and under his fig tree."[4] These are ordinary things. They are domestic, provincial, and routine. The temptation is to think that ordinary life is mundane and meaningless. We feel we could just quit and it wouldn't matter. However, it's precisely here that we so often find the most goodness and the most faithfulness, which are two rare commodities in the world.

Most of the time, we want something different, something out of the ordinary. Certainly, many people are looking for something like that when they come to Africa. The extraordinary definitely has its place, but it seems we more often seek it at the expense of missing the value of the ordinary. All that ordinary stuff feels small and insignificant. It feels like nothing. It is invisible. Yet, Wendell Berry says invisibility is a sign of being at home, which is a very good thing.[5]

〜 〜 〜

Struggles with language are incredibly ordinary for Rachel and me in Burundi. We worked hard to become proficient in French, but most of our patients only speak Kirundi, which has proved to be very challenging to pick up and will likely be the project of a lifetime.

However, the lady in my consultation room now has a different language struggle. She is forty-three years old and a few months ago, her speech got more and more garbled to the point that now she can only grunt. She can understand language. She can write without difficulty. She cannot articulate or pronounce anything. Our surgeon put a scope in her esophagus, and everything looks structurally fine. He sent her to me wondering if she may have a neurological problem.

I'm trying to imagine what it's like to be her, to watch your ability to speak slip away so relentlessly (especially in an oral culture as hers). I ask her to sit on the table so I can check her neurologic function.

I decide to put some of my hard-fought Kirundi skills into practice. "*Fung'amaso.*" I fumble on *close your eyes*, but she gets the idea. I gently touch her forehead. "*Uravyumva?*" Yes, she can feel my touch. Next, I want to see if her mouth muscles have any weakness, so I ask her to smile. In Kirundi, the word for smile (*gutwengatwenga*) is a form of the word for laugh (*gutwenga*). "*Twenga,*" I say.

I think she understands what I'm asking, but her smile bursts through into an embarrassed laugh. Then she continues to laugh.

She is nearly howling, and she can't stop. She puts her head down on her knees and laughs until tears run down her cheeks. Her sister laughs in the nearby chair. The med students laugh. I'm not afraid to chuckle a bit, but I'm glancing around the room for some sign of what the big joke is. I attempt a whole sentence in Kirundi. "*Uratwenga kuber'iki?*" *Why are you laughing?* She looks up at me with a brief pause and then explodes into a fresh round of laughter.

It's unclear at this point where the tears are coming from. Is the great sorrow of these past months finding the path of least resistance? Maybe, but these tears have their fair share of humor as well. There's at least some joy present.

I realize this moment is a great picture of my life. I doubt I can find this woman's diagnosis. Even if I could, I doubt anyone could fix it. Yet, she laughs. Her yellowed teeth are bright against her dark face, and she makes me laugh. Is she laughing because she's embarrassed that I asked her to smile? Are we all laughing at the white guy's attempt to speak Kirundi? I'll never find out for sure, but I'm having a good time nonetheless.

Another day of ordinary sorrow and, in the midst of it, great joy. And often, like right now, I am the random American right in the middle of this mixture, not at all sure what's going on, but finding grace to enjoy the moment nonetheless. This is, more or less, my every day.

This woman's situation could be better. Yes, it could, but it could be worse as well. I wish I could help her more. Nonetheless, I'm quite certain that, when she and her sister return home and her family asks how it went, that along with the tears and frustration, there will also be more laughter.

These pinpricks of golden light so often shine out of the forgettable moments of everyday life. These peals of heart-felt laughter from a woman who can no longer speak a single word are the almost-invisible firstfruits of the promise God has given. In his faithfulness, he will, in the end, keep this promise that "the light shines in the darkness, and the darkness has not overcome it."[6]

≈ ≈ ≈

It is here, in the small and the ordinary, that the best work is done—possibly the only real work. History can be told by recounting great turning points and great leaders, but this is incomplete. All our visions and grand plans are all for naught without those who will steadily and faithfully work it out in ordinary life. Jesus says the kingdom of God is like yeast, slowly and quietly working through all the dough. He says the kingdom is like a tiny mustard seed that grows slowly and unspectacularly to become big enough to have birds perch in its branches.[7] And one ordinary night, silent as the stars and far more invisible to the world around her, a young Jewish girl gave birth to a most extraordinary baby.

In his fantastically fanciful novel *The Book of the Dun Cow*, Walt Wangerin Jr. creates an animal world where the unlikely hero is a rooster that rules his barnyard kingdom from his henhouse, regularly crowing the hours to give a structure and stability to the ordinary lives of the animals.[8] The story goes that God has imprisoned an immense, evil serpent named Wyrm far below the earth's surface. He seethes with anger at his imprisonment, longing to break out and work his destruction in the world, but the thing that really goads him is that the power of his imprisonment lies in the everyday goodness of a bunch of unaware barnyard animals. They don't know it, but the animals are Wyrm's keepers. God, in his wisdom, has done a wonder. The power of the chains of the great Wyrm is in the simple, ordinary, even habitual goodness of a bunch of ignorant animals. It is the ultimate humiliation of evil, and thus it is the glorification of God.

Maybe our world is actually like that. Maybe all the ordinary grace and love is what is really keeping the darkness at bay. At the very least, this idea is consistent with God's strength being glorified in our weakness. For when we have no extraordinary work to contribute, then there is very little in the way of pride and very much in the way of praise for God.

~ ~ ~

All of this encourages me to persevere. More than anything, it gives me peace. I don't need to think that the sum value of my life will be found in extraordinary events and endless variety. I don't need to look at what seems so mundane and small with dismissal and disdain. Robert Farrar Capon says, "It is the ordinary that groans with the unutterable weight of glory."[9] These ordinary moments may be, in fact, the best that I do and the best that is done to me.

QUESTIONS FOR DISCUSSION AND
PERSONAL REFLECTION

1. What does this chapter suggest is the primary promise God offers for the times when it seems like nothing significant is happening? Do you agree, or do you have another way to articulate what God promises?

2. Do you tend to take comfort in the ordinary rhythms of life, or do you tend to become uncomfortable with the mundane? What makes you lean that way?

3. In the moments when you find yourself wishing something significant would happen in your life, ministry, or work, what things might your heart be desiring?

4. In your own life, what elements seem so ordinary, so boring, that you could be underestimating their value and their purpose? What are ways you've seen God work through ordinary, mundane moments, or rhythms?

5. Instead of your own story, think of the stories that surround you. Where might you have overlooked someone or something valuable or important because it seems ordinary or invisible?

8

Haunted

Do not be daunted by the enormity
of the world's grief. Do justly now. Love mercy now.
Walk humbly now. You are not obligated to complete
the work, but neither are you free to abandon it.

—PIRKEI AVOT[1]

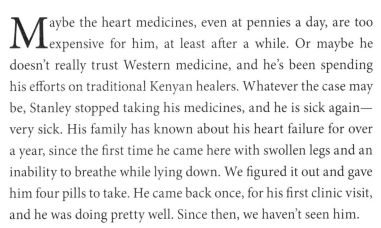

Maybe the heart medicines, even at pennies a day, are too expensive for him, at least after a while. Or maybe he doesn't really trust Western medicine, and he's been spending his efforts on traditional Kenyan healers. Whatever the case may be, Stanley stopped taking his medicines, and he is sick again—very sick. His family has known about his heart failure for over a year, since the first time he came here with swollen legs and an inability to breathe while lying down. We figured it out and gave him four pills to take. He came back once, for his first clinic visit, and he was doing pretty well. Since then, we haven't seen him.

Now, Stanley is in the hospital bed, struggling with his frothy breathing despite a maximum flow of oxygen. He's not that old, but old enough to have a couple grown children around him.

I explain that his blood pressure is low and that this is a bad sign for someone in heart failure because the only available medicines that will help his heart now also have the possibility of lowering his blood pressure further. The options for helping him are seriously limited, but we will try.

After answering a couple questions and making sure the nurses and I are on the same page regarding his treatment plan, I head home. The next morning, when I arrive at the hospital, the overnight staff tells me that he died around two in the morning.

Stanley's is one of a thousand cases that haunt me. It plays around the edges of my imagination. I could have done more. Should I have done more? Would my efforts have made a difference?

I had gone home at a decent hour. What if I had stayed longer? Would I have seen something that could have changed the situation? Something that could have turned Stanley around so he could have gone home and had some more time with his family? What if I had stayed by his bedside all night? When I was an intern in the US, that would have been the expectation for a super-sick guy like this. But here, there is always a super-sick guy, and I can't do that every night. And in any case, if he gets worse, there aren't the same resources available to turn him around. I tell this to myself, and I believe that it's true. Yet, part of me is afraid I'm just trying to justify myself for accepting a lower standard.

Maybe I'm just too lazy and selfish. I know those tendencies are inside me. Am I just letting them rule me? Shouldn't I be putting those things aside? Am I not crucified with Christ, so that it is no longer I who live, but Christ who lives in me?[2]

It's the same nagging question when the intern calls me to discuss a new admission. I put down the phone and think, *She's got it under control. I don't need to walk up to the hospital to see the patient myself. It won't change anything, and the independence is important for her professional growth.* But my heart is conflicted. Am I just saying that because I don't want to go back up there? Because I want to continue doing puzzles on the floor with my daughter? I'm haunted.

Maybe I should spend more time counseling my patients so they have more trust in the recommendations the hospital staff and I make. Maybe I should be working on even more hospital protocols to ensure that, even in the middle of the night, all the staff knows exactly what to do. Maybe I should be out in the villages, instead of the hospital, talking to traditional healers, so their presence wouldn't be such an obstacle to patients' health. Maybe an example of sacrifice will be more important to my family than time spent in relaxing and resting together. If this kind of sacrifice is what God is calling me to do, then he will take care of everything else, right?

Then there are the difficult medical decisions. So often I don't know the right thing to do. What is the diagnosis? Which of the available medicines would be best in this situation? When is it worth asking the patient to spend a lot of money on something that probably won't help, but just maybe will tip the scales?

This doesn't always get easier with time. Mystery patient X comes in this month, and I take my best guess. She doesn't do well. Next month, another one comes in. What do I do now? Unfortunately, there is no answer key to confirm, even after the fact, whether I made the right decision or not. There is no autopsy. There is no pathologist to give me a definitive diagnosis. So I may be just as much in the dark the next time.

Given this situation, shouldn't I be using every ounce of available energy to learn more? I could be better. I am leaving resources untapped. Maybe if I knew more, it would make a difference for these patients.

Haunted.

～ ～ ～

Whenever I go to get groceries in Gitega, thirty minutes away from our home in Burundi, it's always the same scene. A small dirt parking area is next to the grocery store, and I pull the white hatchback Toyota up to the building. I jump out, head into the store, and make my purchases. After paying, a few shop-hands carry the boxes out to the trunk, and I walk back out to the car.

There they are—beggars, closing in on the doors and windows. Emaciated women who are probably widows, holding their young babies. Many of them have obvious physical disabilities. The scars of an old burn glue the wrist down to the forearm, rendering it all but useless. A man walking on his hands, maybe a victim of polio. My wealth is obvious. They saw my boxes of food. They are pleading for a few cents.

The Bible seems to do nothing to assuage this tension. On the contrary, Scripture intensifies the haunting. These beggars are the face of Jesus to me. They are the least of these, and what I do to them, I do to Jesus.[3] "Give to the one who begs from you,"[4] Jesus commands. Yet, if I start, then the crowds will come swarming, and I could stand there all day. What I could give will never be enough. I'm caught between their real and urgent need and a very strong belief that where I am serving at the hospital is a better way to address this problem. Do I really believe that? Is this just more self-justification?

~ ~ ~

I know the counter-arguments. What's more, I believe them ardently. I know limits are necessary for long-term viability in our work. I know God has given me other priorities, such as family and spiritual renewal of my own heart. Even more, I believe much of my tendency to overwork is a manifestation of seeking control and a lack of trust that, in the end, God—not I—will bring about real transformation in this broken world. I believe Burundi will be better sustained by transformed systems than a few street handouts. I believe all these things, and so I agree that limits must be found and maintained.

I'm just never quite sure I've put the limits in the right place. This uncertainty doesn't torture me, but it never quite leaves me alone, either. It's always somewhere in my peripheral vision. Whether I'm sitting down to a good, hot dinner or laughing with friends while playing a game, there is a persistent haunting whisper, *Am I doing enough?*

~ ~ ~

How do we know we've done enough and that our desire to limit ourselves isn't just some justification of laziness or selfishness? When another client calls to over-schedule an appointment because she's having a really hard time, how do we know when to say yes or no? A close friend's daughter is hospitalized for an overdose, and your friend doesn't know what to do. A brother was just diagnosed with a chronic illness, and figuring out how to live now is a daily struggle for him. The community needs a safe place for their schoolchildren in the afternoons, and this new grant could maybe provide that, but we don't have any more time. There is always one more thing. Are we doing enough?

Tim Keller says we are like Oskar Schindler in the movie *Schindler's List*, who after saving so many Jewish lives from the Nazis, condemns himself because he could have done more.[5] He could have sold his car or his lapel pin and saved more people. Each possession he kept was something he could have used to do more. And he didn't. He is overwhelmed by guilt. In the movie, the reaction of the grateful crowd around Schindler is the same as we will get if we try to express these sentiments to others. "No, you've done enough. Look at all you've done." But Schindler is impervious to these reassurances. Why?

Keller argues that most of us would want to say that Schindler's perception of his guilt was misguided. Looking at our own lives, how could we argue otherwise? However, the undeniable truth is he's right. He could have sold his car and saved more Jews. He really could have done more.

～ ～ ～

How can we live amid unending need and not become overwhelmed by guilt? Working more will never suffice. Focusing on the good we have already achieved doesn't address the nagging core question of "should I have done more?" What is the goal underneath the goal? What was Schindler looking for? What are we looking for?

At the end of 1 John 3, in one of the Bible's clearest injunctions to give sacrificially in order to help those in need, there is a mysterious sentence. "If our hearts condemn us, we know that God is greater than our hearts, and he knows everything."[6] Apparently, there is no clear consensus on what exactly that means. However, I know that when I feel that my heart condemns me, it is very good news indeed that God is greater than my heart. Even better news is found when I shift my gaze to the beginning of that chapter. "See what great love the Father has lavished on us, that we should be called children of God! And that is what we are!"[7]

The starting point of John's discussion about love in action is not the needs of others, or guilt, or even personal obedience but rather the love of God. This love is not earned. It's not reluctantly handed over after God has verified that his clipboard is fully checked off. Rather, it is lavished on us, his children. Jesus died for us when we would have none of him, and then God turns and adopts us as his children, giving us the righteousness of Jesus. John's use of multiple exclamation points is well warranted indeed.

So what is my heart seeking? In the middle of these "never-enough" moments, these vague hauntings and misgivings are mixed motives. However, one of my motivations is a desire to feel that I have earned God's approval, or maybe guilt for not having earned it. I need to do more to be worthy enough of God's love. If I can do enough, then my life will be righteous. If I can do enough, I will not need Christ's righteousness (at least, not as much). When anything in this category is my starting place, I will always end up as Oskar Schindler. This feeling of guilt over the inadequacy of my own works is a motivation doomed to strangle me, because the truth is that I am guilty, and I cannot repay enough to make up for all I have done wrong. This is a reality we all must face. What we need is someone "greater than our hearts." So maybe that mysterious phrase in 1 John is a promise we need to remember.

If we, after the model of 1 John 3, make the love of God our starting place rather than our finish line, we find a different paradigm. It may seem asynchronous to turn and remember, in the middle of these haunting thoughts, that God's acceptance is based on the free gift of Christ's righteousness and not on our own works. Nevertheless, it's here that we find both a transformative power and a trustworthy foundation.

I doubt I will ever come to a solid conclusion on these questions. The importance of doing it right and doing enough will probably always leave me in tension. I know I am not the only one. In fact, I have come to believe that absence of this tension would be a dangerous sign of a calloused heart. So one of two things is bound to happen. The tension can loom larger and larger and larger until it makes us despair. Or it can lead us back to a gentle thunder, greater than our condemned hearts, that intones, "Trust in me. Be still. If you are weary and heavy-laden, come to me and rest."

QUESTIONS FOR DISCUSSION AND
PERSONAL REFLECTION

1. What does this chapter suggest is the primary promise God
    offers us when we can't shake the feeling of never having
    done enough? Do you agree, or do you have another way to
    articulate what God promises?
2. In what particular scenarios are you haunted by the idea that
    you have never done enough? How does your heart respond
    in these moments?
3. Have you ever felt like Oskar Schindler? Have you voiced
    these feelings to others? What was their reaction?
4. How does the unmerited nature of God's love for us inform
    these feelings?
5. If the tension of never having done enough doesn't resolve,
    what could be the positive or negative aspects of its persis-
    tence? How might such a tension drive us to God and his
    will? How might an absence of such tension perhaps signify
    a lack of spiritual health?

9

Prayer

Prayer is not a means of removing the unknown and unpredictable elements in life, but rather a way of including the unknown and unpredictable in the outworking of the grace of God in our lives.

—PHILIP YANCEY[1]

❧

Emily says her daughter was fine yesterday. But today, the little three-month-old Kenyan girl is struggling. She's breathing fast. With each breath, the skin below her ribs sucks in. I listen to her lungs. There is nothing to hear—no wheezes, no rattles, just nothing—a dire sign.

The staff and I send her over to the hospital's little ICU. The little baby occupies an adult-sized bed, four feet from a grown man in a coma who sustained a bad head trauma in a motorcycle accident two days ago. To help with the girl's breathing, we set her up with a pressurized breathing mask. It's made for an adult, and it fits her poorly, covering almost her whole face. But it's all we have, and hopefully it will do the trick.

While I'm writing in her chart, one of the nurses tells me Emily herself was extremely sick last year. Sick to the point that, even though she is young, they had decided not to try and resuscitate her if she stopped breathing. No one expected it, but here she is—young and healthy—with a baby no less. Unexpected hope rises, once again.

∼ ∼ ∼

The first night was rocky, and the baby had a hard time keeping her oxygen levels up. The next morning, I need to have a conversation with Emily so she understands how sick her daughter is. She asks me to wait until her husband comes.

A couple hours later, I return to greet her husband. Whereas Emily has retained a certain youthfulness, incredible in light of the stories of her illness, the years wear heavy on her husband. He's probably no more than thirty, thirty-five at the most. His teeth are stained yellow before their time, and several are missing. His body is gaunt, and his face looks tired. He wears a threadbare suit coat, and his pants are several sizes too big.

We sit down in the corner of the ICU to talk. Neither has ever had the luxury of much education, so the nurse translates for me into the local dialect. I tell them we are doing everything we can for their daughter, but if something else gets worse, there isn't much more we can do. Emily's husband eagerly drinks in my words, intently looking me in the eyes, even though it is the nurse's words he understands.

When we finish, as I often do in these situations, I ask if I can pray with them. They agree, and immediately seize both my hands and the hands of my nurse, forming a tight circle of four. Their heads are bowed, and the nurse and I exchange a surprised glance. Normally, patients are glad to accept an offer of prayer, but they are more or less passive in the event. I offer a prayer in English, that God would save this child and sustain these parents. I finish and attempt to withdraw my hands, but they don't let go. Without looking up, Emily's husband launches into a prayer in Kalenjin, rattling off his petitions to the "amens" of his wife. His words are punctuated by the shaking of our combined fists. When he finishes, Emily starts. They continue for several minutes, finally concluding with a long "amen" that comes out like a sigh.

They thank me and immediately head to the foot of their daughter's bed. Dad is on the right, between the bed and the wall, and Mom is on the left, in between her daughter and the man with the head trauma. Eyes closed, still voicing their prayers out loud, still pumping their fists. That is how I leave them: zealous petitions and repetitive chants. They seem confident that they are being heard—heard by the God who spared Emily's life last year, heard by the God who has brought them through poverty and lack of opportunity to this very moment.

It strikes me that, if these parents had more education, they might be researching their daughter's diagnosis on their mobile phones, seeking reassurance that their daughter is receiving the right treatment, and arming themselves with information, like a veneer of control.

If they were more socially connected, they would probably be out on the veranda with the men whose suits aren't so thread-bare, texting their numerous relations to gather financial and social support during this time.

These parents are instead interceding, standing in the gap for their little girl, for this is who they are. They are the widow tossing her two copper coins into the basket. They are giving what they have.[2]

~ ~ ~

About a year after this scene in the Kenyan ICU, I am in the United States speaking at a church about our plans to move to Burundi. I speak of the needs there and invite people to get involved. After the service, I have a little table in the lobby with pictures and a sign-up sheet for our newsletter. People come by and chat. There's a bit of a queue, and it's a while before they all go their own way.

When only a couple people are still around, I notice a lady in her forties sitting on a bench watching me. When I glance at her, she catches my eyes and makes a gesture to let me know she's just waiting until I'm done talking with all the other people.

When they are gone, I go over to her. She says she's waiting because her friend is sick in the hospital. She doesn't understand the whole situation, and so she isn't able to give me any significant details. During the service, while I was sharing, she thought she would ask me to pray for her friend. Because I'm a doctor, I would know how to pray for her. I would understand all those things that she doesn't understand. I can pray in a way she can't.

Well, at this point, I'm flush with the past forty-five minutes of shaking hands with people and talking about my life. I'm full of hearing how I am doing such great work. Despite a distant sense that something's off, I tell her I will gladly pray for her. I pray for her friend and her friend's medical team. I pray for her unknown illness. I have a vague feeling I haven't yet said anything professional, so I try to throw in some medical words so she would be confirmed in her belief that I knew something she didn't.

She thanks me warmly. She looks at the stack of picture cards and the email sign-up sheet. She says she doesn't have an email address but writes down her street address, in case I ever mail something.

~ ~ ~

The Norwegian pastor Ole Hallesby writes that prayer is fundamentally helplessness: "To pray is nothing more involved than to let Jesus into our needs."[3] We are not trying to convince God of something, nor are we trying to get his attention. We are asking for God's hand in all we cannot do. We are not trying to strategize or fix things. We don't have to come up with ideas for God to consider or ways he might want to answer our prayers. Rather we are simply bringing to God our insufficiencies. We are there to place our inadequacy in his hands, precisely because we know our hands are insufficient.

Hallesby points to Mary, the mother of Jesus, at the wedding of Cana as someone who prays well. She has a need, namely the embarrassing lack of wine. Mary knows to take this need to Jesus, since he is never less than equal to the situation. She speaks four simple words, "They have no wine."[4] Mary is no expert on how to solve the problem. She suggests no course of action, and even if she had, it is doubtful she would have suggested turning water into wine. Yet, Mary seems at peace with her part of the story, for she says no more.

When I remember the mom and dad flanking the bedside of their baby girl's hospital bed, I must admit I have no idea what they were saying. Maybe they were claiming promises. Maybe they were repeating some formula they had heard their pastor say. Maybe they were reminding God of what he had done for the mom. I don't know. They certainly spoke more words than Mary. But I have no doubt that, underneath it all, they were praying precisely because of their helplessness, and they knew to whom they could direct their prayers.

When I think about the lady in the American church, I don't regret that I agreed to pray for her friend. Nevertheless, I wish I had taken the chance to tell her she already knows how to pray for her friend. In fact, she was far more in touch with her own helplessness in the situation than I was. I regret that I allowed her to persist in the idea that my professional background would give me any inkling on how to pray for her. Sure, I can make a guess at what her doctors are thinking. But that has nothing to do with praying for her. God already understands all of that much better than I. Somewhere in the back of my mind, I knew this. But she had put me up on the pedestal, and I guess I didn't want to get down. It was easy to stay there. Instead, I wish I had told her I would gladly pray with her, but only as another beggar, not as a doctor with some kind of superior prayer knowledge.

~ ~ ~

We often imagine we pray from our strength, just as we imagine God's power will be made perfect in our strength. Nevertheless, that promise belongs to our weakness,[5] to all the parts of our hearts and lives that we would rather hide. In weakness, we need just such a promise as we are given.

God doesn't need suggested plans or certain key details brought into the center of his attention. We pray because we need. We pray because we can do nothing else. That means the more we see the truth of our neediness, of our insufficiency, the more we will pray. If we were to see the whole truth, we would pray all the time.

I wrote in chapter 5 about how my daughter wanted to pray for Emmanuel, and how his recovery was an unexpected story of hope for me. Since then, I've made a habit of asking my kids to pray for my patients. It has led to some interesting bedtime conversations, but I must say that it has also correlated with a striking number of unexpected recoveries.

"The prayer of a righteous person is powerful and effective."[6] I memorized this verse when I was a teenager. I'm not sure what I thought it meant. Maybe I thought it meant people who followed God's commands really well could pray and their prayers would change things more than the prayers of someone who didn't follow God's commands as well. The problem is this interpretation divorces this verse from the rest of the New Testament's concept of righteousness. The only righteousness I have is that which is given freely by God because of his unmerited love, and definitively not by my following of God's commands. This verse, thus, promises Christians that our prayers are powerful because they originate in our fundamental nature as those who are now righteous in Christ. In fact, recognizing that our only righteousness comes from Christ reminds us of our helplessness and thus pushes us to prayer.

I see a similar phenomenon when I think about my kids. I believe their prayers are heard, but not because of their obedience to God's commands. I believe their prayers are heard because they are my kids, and I love them. I can't imagine not wanting to listen to them praying for someone who is suffering. Maybe God feels the same way about me, which is the love that made him sacrifice so much to make me righteous. Maybe that's the same love that gives my prayers whatever power they may have.

For most Christians, any discussion on prayer quickly provokes guilt in everyone for having neglected prayer. We resolve to pray more and habitually fail rapidly to keep that resolve. The under-emphasized question is, Why? Why don't we pray more? Do we not think we're being heard? Do we not think God, though he obviously encourages prayer, will act any differently because of our prayers?

Maybe that's part of it, but I think the biggest reason we don't pray is that we really don't think we need to. The proof for this is found in how our prayerfulness changes in moments of true desperation. Put me in a situation where I obviously can't solve the situation, and I don't have to be goaded into prayer. It pours naturally out of my neediness. Let the storm calm down a bit, and I stop praying as soon as I think I can navigate the waters.

If the root of the problem is that we seem unable to see our true neediness, then maybe we can start there. We can repent and confess our utter incapacity to rightly see our incapacity. We can cry out with our fellow blindman, "Jesus, Son of David, have mercy on me!"[7]

~ ~ ~

Two days after their first prayers in the ICU, the three-month-old daughter died. She just never got any better, and she could only keep up that level of respiratory distress for so long.

I don't know what her parents thought. I never knew what they prayed, but I would guess their prayers, at least in part, were not answered. I do not doubt they were heard. The prayers of the

weak in their weakness—these are gathered and treasured. These
are heard—but not always answered.

Heard but not answered—is that enough? Is this sufficient to
keep me praying for the next little three-month-old that is under
my care? Is it enough for any of us in the teeth of the next tragedy
that hits us? Is that enough for these two parents?

Jesus seems to understand this as the crux of the matter
because much of his teaching on prayer centers on perseverance,
such as the man who keeps knocking on his neighbor's door in
the middle of the night, until he gets up and gives him what he
wants.[8] There is the widow who wears down the unjust judge
with her persistence until he uncharacteristically grants her justice.[9] Then there are the heartbreakingly unrelenting appeals of
the Syrophoenician woman for the healing of her daughter.[10] She
is utterly shameless and would rather identify with a dog under a
table seeking crumbs than turn her prayer away from Jesus.

Frederick Buechner sums it up like this:

> What about when the boy is not healed? When, listened
> to or not listened to, the prayer goes unanswered? Who
> knows? Just keep praying, Jesus says. Remember the
> sleepy friend, the crooked judge. Even if the boy dies,
> keep on beating the path to God's door, because the one
> thing you can be sure of is that down the path you beat
> with even your most half-cocked and halting prayer the
> God you call upon will finally come, and even if he does
> not bring you the answer you want, he will bring you
> himself. And maybe at the secret heart of all our prayers
> that is what we are really praying for.[11]

All this leaves those of us who pray with a terrible mystery. We are called to trust in some bigger promise, some perspective that is bigger than our own, in which all our unanswered prayers are knitted together into something beautiful. But for now, this fulfillment is unseen, and hope may be scarce. Yet there is a heart's cry beneath the heart's cry. Underneath it all, we yearn for the presence of the one who is himself Life and Healing. He has come, and he promises to come again. He has shown his love and his faithfulness. So, if he's the one who hears prayers, and if he's the one who promises, then maybe we have reason enough to continue to pray.

QUESTIONS FOR DISCUSSION AND
PERSONAL REFLECTION

1. What does this chapter suggest is the primary promise God offers us when we fear our prayers won't be answered? Do you agree, or do you have another way to articulate what God promises?

2. Describe a time when prayer felt futile, unimportant, or otherwise non-essential. Why did it feel that way? How did that affect the way in which you engaged with the situation? How did the situation end?

3. Our attitudes toward prayer can reveal our central beliefs about what we see as God's role in our lives and work. If you don't pray as much as you want to (which is most of us), why not? What are you believing that doesn't encourage (or maybe frankly discourage) prayer?

4. Second Chronicles 20:12 prays, "We do not know what to do, but our eyes are on you." How does the Norwegian pastor Ole Hallesby's definition of prayer as helplessness strike you? Try praying for one week without suggesting a solution to God, just presenting your needs. What was the experience like? How did it change your posture toward God and the brokenness around you?

5. How do you react to the notion that the end result of our prayers might not be the resolution we are asking for, but rather, knowing God more? Does this feel more like a comfort or a cop-out? Why?

10

Mystery

*I could probably not say more than
that life is a very deep mystery, and that finally
the grace of God is all that can resolve it.
And the grace of God is also a very deep mystery.*

—MARILYNNE ROBINSON[1]

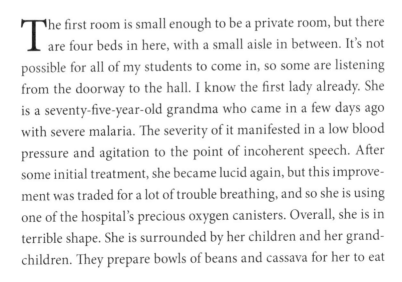

The first room is small enough to be a private room, but there are four beds in here, with a small aisle in between. It's not possible for all of my students to come in, so some are listening from the doorway to the hall. I know the first lady already. She is a seventy-five-year-old grandma who came in a few days ago with severe malaria. The severity of it manifested in a low blood pressure and agitation to the point of incoherent speech. After some initial treatment, she became lucid again, but this improvement was traded for a lot of trouble breathing, and so she is using one of the hospital's precious oxygen canisters. Overall, she is in terrible shape. She is surrounded by her children and her grandchildren. They prepare bowls of beans and cassava for her to eat

in the moments when her breathing isn't so labored. Her husband passed away just a couple days ago, also from a bad case of
malaria. The family is grieving, and they are afraid to tell their
grandmother the news. The sorrow of the situation is evident,
but to me, it is tempered a bit by seeing the fullness of the woman's life all around her. Whatever happens, any Burundian would
say she has been blessed.

The next room is one I always jokingly refer to as the "Ward
of Darkness," due to its lack of windows and our frequent power
outages. A new patient is here, a thirty-one-year-old woman who
delivered a baby three weeks ago. She also started having trouble
breathing, so her local clinic sent her straight to the hospital.

Unlike most of our patients, she looks strong, well fed, and
healthy. But something has gone wrong, and now she is floridly
infected with something we can't identify. Her temperature soars,
and her blood pressure drops. The interns and I have started her
on antibiotics and lots of IV fluids. We decide to do some more
tests and broaden her medicines.

The next day, her fever isn't relenting, and she is getting
weaker and weaker. Her newborn baby is lying on the bed, nursing from her mother who doesn't have the strength to rise, and
whose milk supply is rapidly diminishing. Her husband is by her
bedside, and we see him throughout the day, carrying their baby
through the halls. Our team talks more. We rack our brains for
every diagnosis we could possibly treat. We treat her even for the
things for which her tests are negative. We check on the baby and
find a tin of baby formula. Then the mother dies.

Back in the first room, the elderly widow slowly stabilizes.
Over the course of several days, we decrease her oxygen, and she
tolerates it well. On her last day, she smiles at me, thanking me

and shaking my hand with both of hers. Her children express their gratitude.

It's all so very juxtaposed. The young, healthy mother with a family and a dependent newborn baby slips away while the elderly widow beats the odds to go home once again. Why would this happen?

Then again, the widow's family had just lost a father, so though she may be ancient by Burundian standards, maybe it's better for the family to be spared the tragedy of losing two parents in the same week.

～ ～ ～

These things are just utterly impossible to weigh out. And yet I try. I try to make some kind of sense of them by looking at them from different angles, trying to see how the light might outweigh the darkness. My only conclusion is that I will never see deep enough into the mystery of our manifold world to be able to make a call one way or another. Why does tragedy strike one and not another? Who knows? Who knows what just happened here? We tried our best. We found great sorrow, but we also found some great joy and beauty, as well. But what is the sum of it all? When we put all the pieces together, what is the dominant story being told? Any pretense on my part to be empiric in one judgment or another would be the height of foolishness. Who knows?

～ ～ ～

About a week later, I'm back in morning prayer at the hospital. Despite my straining attention, I miss the announcement of the Scripture reading in Kirundi, so I look at my friend's Bible next to me. We are reading from Isaiah 6. It's a classic missionary motivation text, one I've heard more times than I can remember. Isaiah has a vision of the glory of God's throne room, and he hears God ask, "Whom shall I send, and who will go for us?" Isaiah says, "Here am I! Send me."

For the first time, I was struck by the message that immediately follows, "'Go, say to this people: 'Keep on hearing, but do not understand; keep on seeing, but do not perceive.' Make the heart of this people dull, and their ears heavy, and blind their eyes . . . until cities lie waste without inhabitant, and houses without people, and the land is a desolate waste.'"[2]

That is Isaiah's mission? That is the message? He is supposed to go and tell people their comprehension and wisdom will be lessened? Why bother telling them, if we have already established that they're an uncomprehending people? The mission seems so incredibly incongruous. Why would he be sent to say that? It had to be a mystery to Isaiah. However, if Isaiah was surprised, he gives no indication of being so. Maybe he had been surprised one too many times already. Or maybe he had seen the Lord, and what exactly he was going to do was not as important as the one who had commissioned him. At any rate, he stares at the mystery, and he says, "Okay." He responds with faith.

~ ~ ~

When the depth of the mystery surrounding me is unveiled, I'm called to have faith, which is a concept that has long given me pause. Frankly, it's given me confusion at certain times as well. It's helpful for me to think of faith in two ways. One meaning of faith is belief in the truth of a given idea or fact. In this sense, I have belief-faith in gravity, mathematics, and that George Washington was the first President of the United States. I also have belief-faith that God exists, that Jesus is the Son of God incarnate, and that he bodily rose from the dead. Though belief-faith for anything is never 100 percent certain, all people have good reasons for the things they believe. Christianity asks us not for blind faith. Rather we are called to recognize that, though nothing in this world is ever free from doubt, what Christianity proclaims offers far more reason to believe it than not to.

The second meaning of faith is trust. This trust-faith is directed, not toward an idea or a fact, but toward someone. I have trust-faith in my wife, in my longtime friend, in the leader of a certain organization, and in God. When I say people are faithful, I mean they are trustworthy. Even if they were to do something I didn't understand, I would not immediately assume of them malfeasance or corruption. I would instead trust that they see a bigger story than I do, and they are acting in a way somehow consistent with the character I have come to know of them.

This is the kind of faith God is seeking in the Bible. This trust-faith is also a virtue. It is a choice, though not an uninformed one. The Bible gives people many reasons that God is trustworthy, the pinnacle being when he gave himself up to sin and death for us in the person of Jesus.

~ ~ ~

The sixty-year-old man in the bed before me is certainly a mystery. He had a big stroke a couple of years ago, but he mostly recovered. A few days ago, he inexplicably slipped into a coma. He has a fever, and his blood pressure is very high. The list of what might be wrong is long, and the hospital's diagnostic capacity is not up to the task. After a week, he isn't improving, and the remaining options for treatment feel like last-ditch efforts. I'm not sure what his family thinks about continuing treatment after so little progress, so I go back after rounds to speak with his wife.

I haven't talked much with her previously, but her constant presence and her poise have been noticed. She quickly dismisses my student's Kirundi translation, saying she can understand my French.

I start from the beginning, explaining all the difficulties that we're having in treating her husband. I point out the lack of progress despite all our efforts, and I try to lay out the options, stumbling somewhat to find the appropriate cross-cultural and cross-linguistic way to express that I'm not sure it's worth starting new treatments.

She listens calmly as I alternately explain and bumble along. She is attentive and never interrupts. When I finally stop, she says, "But you must remember that there is a good God. He can do anything. You must remember that. He can do *anything.*"

"Amen," I say. "And God loves your husband."

"Yes, he loves him!" she continues. "He has protected him for sixty years! We will see what happens, but you go ahead and do what you think is good. God will do it."

We pray together, asking God to do what we cannot, to protect a man he has protected through so many past troubles. We ask God to help us trust during these difficult times.

As we walk out of the room, I say to my student, "Well, she is a strong woman. Much stronger than me." My student laughs.

~ ~ ~

Occasionally, I have seen similar responses from both Africans and Americans. In the face of overwhelmingly terminal disease, some people will persist in saying not only that God *can* heal them but that he *will*. Personally, that's hard for me to relate to. I honestly don't know what God will do, and I've seen way too much to say otherwise.

Such words look like denial. Sometimes they are. Sometimes they are nothing but a cover-up for fear. But I don't think they always have to be. Sometimes, these words can be a response of faith in the face of mystery. When I was in college, I had an elderly friend named Janice who was dying of cancer. She said over and over again that God was going to heal her. She never permitted any alternative. Her cancer got worse and worse. Even when the doctors stopped the chemotherapy, she said God was going to heal her. She was bedridden and intermittently confused. During a lucid period, someone spoke to her about God healing her, and she said, "Don't you see? He has already done it." She was right, and she died in peace.

Janice wasn't in denial. She was defying death. Her cancer took her life, but there was resurrection waiting. I don't think that, anywhere along that road, death's sting ever took hold of her. Maybe that's the difference between denial and defiance— the difference, in the face of mystery, between the response of fear and the response of faith. When life doesn't go how we hoped, when the disease starts spiraling in every direction, the response of faith can still embrace these disappointments as a situation where God is still present. The undesired and unanticipated circumstances don't cause faith to recoil and say, "But I *knew* you were going to heal me! Why did you let me down?" Trust can persevere in the face of mystery because of a hope in a story bigger than what's visible and because of the continued trustworthiness of God who's shaping this story.

I do have faith that God is true to his promises. Somehow, he is taking all the orphaned threads of countless frayed lives and weaving them into a tapestry that is larger and more beautiful than anyone can imagine. Sometimes, I can see a bit with my own eyes. Sometimes, I can't, and so I have to trust. Sometimes, I cling to past evidences of God's goodness to give me strength because the mystery is deep.

I cannot grasp it all, nor can I anticipate it all—no one can. We cannot let our limited perspective paralyze us into inaction, but we do need to recognize that there is more to the story than we can ever comprehend.

What are we doing? Where are we going? How does it all fit together? Who knows? God knows. If that was all we had, it would be enough.

QUESTIONS FOR DISCUSSION AND
PERSONAL REFLECTION

1. What does this chapter suggest is the primary promise God offers us when we cannot understand what God is doing? Do you agree, or do you have another way to articulate what God promises?

2. Describe a time when it was hard to trust God for what he was doing in someone with whom you were walking. From where did the difficulty stem? How did the situation end?

3. How would you describe faith to someone who does not come from a Christian background?

4. Imagine someone you know is in need and says to you, "I don't just pray that God will change this. I *know* he will!" What is the reaction of your heart to this situation? What could be going on in his/her heart?

5. Describe a current situation that you cannot understand God would allow. Then, imagine that no more light is ever shed on the story to justify or explain what has happened. Though the mystery remains, what are some possible ways in which God could be redeeming that brokenness?

11

Suffering

The one who does not see God's suffering
does not see his love. God is suffering love. So suffering
is down at the center of things, deep down where the
meaning is. Suffering is the meaning of our world.
For Love is the meaning. And Love suffers.
The tears of God are the meaning of history.

—NICOLAS WOLTERSTORFF[1]

❧

It is my very first time in Africa, during my final year of medical school, and I am spending two months in a rural hospital in northwestern Zambia. Everything is so new to me—the dry dirt roads and the hospital that keeps running despite the power outages. For the first time, I see in person the exotic, tropical diseases and the old medicines I have only read about in books. An unprecedented amount of suffering surrounds me. A young lady has a tumor the size of a basketball that has been destroying her knee for the past year. The child I had been seeing every day for the past week isn't here anymore. He died during the night.

Wailing mothers are crying out between their sobs for the children they have lost. I can hear them all the way in my apartment.

Then, one day after rounds, my supervising doc tells me a new trauma patient has arrived, and he wants me to evaluate her. As I walk across the room, I can see two nurses wheeling in someone on a stretcher. At a near distance, I can see a beautiful face with eyes closed—a young woman who could be sleeping but for all the blood.

The nurses tell me the story as they work to get an IV started, and I search for a pulse. Her name is Alice, and when she was fourteen, she was married to a man who turned out to be quite violent. He would beat her habitually. That was five years ago. The other night, she finally decided she'd had enough, and she ran away. Her tyrant of a husband got high on some local herb and ran after her—with an axe.

Now, her skull is fractured in at least four places, and she has numerous axe cuts on her head and hands, where she tried to fend off his blows. Presumably, he stopped because he thought she was dead, which was a reasonable assumption by the look of her. But he was wrong, at least for the moment. Someone found her and brought her several hours away to the hospital. Now, she's lying here in front of me, unconscious and bloody.

I'm frozen inside. My gloved hands continue through their machinations to get some vital signs on her, but on the inside, I am stunned into silence. I have travelled across the world believing that caring for people in Jesus's name is better than caring for them without Jesus, but does Jesus have anything to offer to this brutality? Is there anything in this world that can stand up to such wickedness?

~ ~ ~

The blinding reality is that suffering is everywhere. The world is filled with trouble, disease, and loss. Bodies break and waste away. Loved ones are lost, along with the opportunities to love them better. Our attempts to love and be loved are thwarted, and we end up flinging our words at one another like spears. We suffer, and we cause suffering based on what we do and what we leave undone. Maybe we regret it afterward, but we are aching so much from our own injuries that we prefer to save our pity and compassion for ourselves. We hurt. We suffer.

Since moving to Africa, there's probably no single theme that has felt so urgent to me. No other problem has felt so pressing: if I can't find some way to at least think about all the suffering around me, then I won't last long here. I've already told these stories of suffering—the children, mothers, fathers, families, and villages. Hunger, pain, disability, and death are everywhere. How can we go forward with all this suffering? I knew it could be bad, but feeling how pervasive and destructive suffering really is has challenged me on a whole new level. Where is God in all this suffering? Is there any promise that can sustain us?

If we walk into the dark places of the world, then our encounters with suffering are inevitable. If we want to be present when we can help, then we must also be present when we can't. We can't know ahead of time whom we can help. Sometimes, we can make a great impact. Other times, we can't. The two are inextricably linked, and situations don't sort themselves out ahead of time into categories of "able to help" and "unable to help." We follow Jesus into the darkness, and it is here that the light can shine the brightest. However, in the same places where the victories are the most dramatic, the magnitude and frequency of the tragedies go up in a seemingly proportional manner. So, what can we do in the face of all these sorrowful realities?

~ ~ ~

We can plainly start by jettisoning one false promise that manages to cling to our world despite its patent lie. It goes like this, "You will not have to suffer as long as you have enough faith and do what is right." This fallacy can be descriptively called the "incomplete equation of retributive justice,"[2] and I suppose I will always be drawn to it whenever I mistakenly consider myself just. Christianity never promises that those who put their faith in God are exempt from suffering, and biblical examples of this are blindingly obvious. We throw this falsehood overboard, only to find in the morning that it has found a way back to society and even to little dark corners of our own hearts.

This idea that those who are faithful will not suffer goes back, at least, to the story of Job, which scholars think is a very old story, even by biblical standards. The book of Job is forty-two chapters of wisdom and enigma, all mixed up together. Strangely, about half of the book is poetic recitations of erring wisdom by Job's so-called friends. Though those lies can sound eerily true, I am still mystified why the story spends so much time on them. But at the center of it all is Job—suffering Job.

The outline of the story goes like this: Job was righteous and prosperous. God allows Satan to cause the loss of Job's wealth, family, reputation, and health. The immediate reason for this is God wanting to make a point to Satan, but readers get the feeling that God is making a point to them as well.

Job sits in agony, scraping broken shards of pottery over his open sores when his three friends arrive. They sit silently with him for seven days before speaking, which just goes to show that it's never too late to say exactly the wrong thing. All three friends have roughly the same message: Job is suffering; therefore, he needs to repent of the sin that brought God's judgment on him. The innocent do not suffer.

This is the only argument that Job's friends can allow, at least from the safe perspective of their own healthy bodies and unravaged lives. Job refuses to admit that his unrighteousness could be the cause of his suffering and demands to present his case before God. When Job's friends finally decide they can no longer argue with him, Elihu, a younger, more feisty observer, jumps in and continues the same argument, which just goes to show we can never be too old or too young to share in this kind of folly.

Then, God shows up. At this point, I would expect God to tell Job about Satan's test and to congratulate Job on his faithfulness. But God doesn't. Instead, he fires off his own few chapters of poetry, the theme of which is the puniness of Job and the incomparable awesomeness of God. Job is overwhelmed by God's glory and recants. God tells Job's friends they were wrong and as a seeming afterthought, readers learn that Job prospered again.

The whole story could be condensed into this interaction:

Job: "I am suffering, and I want to know why, God!"

God: "Where were you when I laid the foundations of the earth?"

Job: "I am satisfied."

The obvious absence is that God never answers Job's questions. An answer existed, and oddly, as the readers, we know what it was, namely this showdown between God and Satan. But we have a new question—how could Job never learn this and yet be satisfied? Job wanted to know why. He doesn't learn it, and he doesn't seem to care any longer.

Why is this? I think it's because the real question is not, "Why is this happening?" or "What is the reason for all this suffering?" Many people think "Why?" is the question that matters the most, but the story of Job suggests otherwise—so do the Psalms of lament. The real questions are, "God, are you there?" and "God, do you care for me?"[3] And these two questions might just be one single question at the end, where God's presence and his love are found to be inextricable.

Maybe our desire to know why is just a means of knowing God's presence. We ask, "Why" because we seek a reason that can show us God is present and his love is with us. We hope that such a reason will be like a proxy for his presence. However, Job found God's presence without a reason for his suffering and reached a satisfaction that probably surpassed that of a mere proxy.

Buechner puts it like this:

As for the children he had lost when the house blew down, not to mention all his employees, he never got an explanation about them because he never asked for one, and the reason he never asked for one was that he knew that even if God gave him one that made splendid sense out of all the pain and suffering that had ever been since the world began, it was no longer splendid sense that he needed because with his own eyes he had beheld, and not as a stranger, the one who in the end clothed all things, no matter how small or confused or in pain, with his own splendor. And that was more than sufficient.[4]

When we suffer, questions can naturally overwhelm us. When we walk with others who suffer, it's the same. We want to know "Why?" or "What is God doing?" Or maybe we're not sure what we're asking, but we are sure what we want to say ends with a question mark.

But God comes to us. In our suffering. With Jesus, suffering is revolutionized in a way Job couldn't have believed, though it would add glory to the unsurpassable glory that had already filled him. God came, and he suffered—for us and because of love.

~ ~ ~

After Alice's IV is in place, the nurses decide to move her to the operating room to wash out her head wounds. As they wheel her away, words from a very old hymn come to mind:

"O sacred head, now wounded, with grief and shame bowed down."[5]

~ ~ ~

For several years before Alice came into the emergency room, I had been struggling with the idea of the suffering God. The uniqueness of it is indisputable. No one else tells such a story. God comes to earth to suffer and die, in pain and injustice. God carries scars on his hands and feet. There's no other God like that. I understood that, because Jesus died and was resurrected, we had an open door to forgiveness and eternal life. But what bearing does that door have upon our suffering? We still suffer, and how does that change anything for us now? People seemed to find the idea of the suffering God significant, but I couldn't understand what meaning it imparted. Probably because it isn't the kind of meaning that's understood by a well-articulated syllogism. It's understood by experiencing its reality.

Because God has come and suffered, Alice was not lost in some kind of primordial pioneer wasteland. Someone had walked that same path before her. And not just anyone—God. His head was wounded. He bore shame and grief. Alice, even if unaware, was walking the path that God had walked.

So now, suffering is holy ground. Every year, pilgrims flock to the Middle East to walk the land where Jesus walked. I have not yet been among them, but I can easily grasp the appeal of walking among the hills and towns that the Son of God walked. The very idea that he traveled these roads . . . the same that I am walking on now! Maybe a vial of the dirt there won't cause miracles in some distant cathedral, but the significance is still easy to grasp. It is holy ground.

Yet, it wasn't just physical dirt that Jesus trod. He walked the paths of suffering and injustice. He knows the pain of violence and hatred and all their blood-soaked consequences. He voluntarily put himself in a place where suffering and injustice and forsakenness equally apply to him as they do to us. Again, Buechner says, "For the sake of the one who bore it before they did, we are to honor [those who suffer] for the sanctity of their burden. For [H]is sake, we are called to see their terrible beauty."[6]

Alice survived that attack. She was washed up and stitched together and given lots of IV antibiotics. Her face swelled up beyond recognition, but then she woke up and slowly began to heal. The day before she left the hospital, someone took a picture of her. In it, she is looking back at the camera with steady, clear eyes which, at least for the moment, hold no fear. The swelling is gone, and there is even a hint of a smile. Because her wounds were mostly in her scalp, the only noticeable thing about her appearance is several straight white lines that emerge about an inch from her hairline onto her forehead.

Scars—we all have them. Some scars are on the inside, and some are on the outside. Often, we try to hide them. But our Savior has scars as well. I suppose he could have gotten rid of them with his newly resurrected body, but he didn't. He displays them, and he calls us to look upon them.

Steve Saint said once that the world is looking for people who have scars in the same places where the world now has wounds.[7]

Maybe that's why it matters.

QUESTIONS FOR DISCUSSION AND
PERSONAL REFLECTION

1. What does this chapter suggest is the primary promise God offers us in the face of tremendous suffering? Do you agree, or do you have another way to articulate what God promises?

2. Describe a time when immense suffering in someone else has shocked you to the point of questioning God's relevance or his presence. What made that particular situation so challenging?

3. That God himself has suffered and died is unique to Christianity. What real difference has this made to you when you have suffered? Or to someone else that you have known when he/she suffered? How would you describe the relevance of Jesus's suffering to someone who is not a Christian?

4. In your experience walking with those in need, what are the questions you often hear directed toward God? Do you think there are questions underneath those questions? Are there other questions that they're not asking that may be more important?

5. If we see in Jesus's glorified, resurrection body the firstfruits of his promise to make all things new, why do his scars remain? As you reflect on this, what does it mean to you?

12

Consolation

Compassion asks us to go where it hurts,
to enter into the places of pain, to share in brokenness,
fear, confusion and anguish . . . Compassion requires
us to be weak with the weak, vulnerable with the
vulnerable, and powerless with the powerless.

—*COMPASSION: A REFLECTION ON THE CHRISTIAN LIFE*[1]

Morning rounds start with prayer. It's usually roughly the same prayer every day. An ordinary litany, another trodding over a well-worn path. The medical students, the nurses, the nursing students, and I gather around. We pray for wisdom in all the decisions before us. We pray we would act in love and show the light of Jesus. I pray all the students would gain knowledge and skills that will serve their current and future patients. We remember we are ultimately counting on God to heal the patients he loves so much. Then, we begin.

We usher out in a great cloud of white coats. I let the nurses and students direct me, and they lead me first to the bed of a four-month-old baby. Her mother brought her in three days ago with terrible trouble breathing. The baby is gasping so badly she is unable to breastfeed, and so the hospital staff has been gingerly giving the baby some IV fluids in addition to antibiotics for a presumed pneumonia.

The students bring me here first for two reasons. One, the baby is doing poorly despite our maximal therapy. We have a single individual oxygen concentrator against the wall, the kind that someone who is dependent on home oxygen therapy would keep by their bedside in the United States. Someone at the hospital ingeniously spliced pieces of old stethoscope tubing together to split the oxygen delivery into two or three routes so we can give oxygen to multiple children at a time. There are still children who have to go without, but not this baby. Nevertheless, even with supplemental oxygen, we can't get her oxygen up to a satisfactory level. She is still breathing over seventy times a minute, her ribs retracting in with each labored breath. She is not doing well, but I don't think we can do anything else other than hope we can keep supporting her until her body recovers.

The second reason we're starting with this baby is that her mom wants to go home. This is a common request, but a bit unusual for a baby who is in such desperate shape. I ask why. Her mom tells me her friend told her the baby needs her uvula cut out of the back of her throat. Her friend told her they don't know about this treatment at hospitals, but this is what her baby needs now.

This is not the first time I've heard of this village medical practice. In fact, we've seen a number of cases come into the hospital when the practice has gone bad. I tell the mom that, though I recognize her daughter is not doing well, I simply cannot advise that she go home for this or any other reason—she will not survive very long without oxygen. This conversation goes back and forth a few times. Mom acquiesces, and we pray together for her and the child. We pray for healing and for understanding.

Twenty minutes later, while I am still in the same room, about three beds down the line, one of the nurses gently asks for my attention. I step out of the great white coat cloud, and she tells me the baby from the first bed is no longer breathing. I quickly step over and confirm the child has died.

I defer to my Burundian colleagues about the best way to handle what comes next. As usual, they ask Mom and Dad to come quickly across the hall, out of the big ward and into a private office. We sit down, and the nurse delivers the news quietly to the parents.

Before the nurse has finished, Mom shrieks and falls down on the floor. She throws an old terrycloth towel over her head and begins to writhe and wail. I look up to her husband and see tears in his eyes, which is extremely unusual for this culture. He is struggling to keep his composure as he spurts out some rapid Kirundi. The only thing I can catch is the phrase "build a family" repeated several times. Among the nurses are sounds of regret and reproach.

I ask what he said. He said this is the second baby who has died. Their first died at six and a half months old, also here at the hospital. And now the second has died at four months. They have no living children. In traditional African cultures, a woman's worth is tied to her ability to have a family. He wants to have a family, and so he sees no other choice than to leave his wife and take a new wife.

After several rounds back and forth with the nurses, the father changes his mind and says he will not send his wife away.

Then, for the first time, words come out from under the towel. The wife says it doesn't matter. She has too much shame. She can never go back to her village.

~ ~ ~

At the beginning of 2 Corinthians, Paul writes that God "comforts us in all our affliction, so that we may be able to comfort those who are in any affliction, with the comfort with which we ourselves are comforted by God."[2] Our calling is clear. We have been given comfort, and part of that comfort's purpose is to comfort others in their affliction—any affliction.

The call is clear, but the application can feel like utter impossibility. I'm sitting on the bench next to a sobbing Burundian father, and his wife is still laying on the floor, her wailing now reduced to despair. They came here looking to save their daughter, and it didn't happen. The result is not just loss—which is overwhelming enough on its own—but also shame and stigma. I feel trapped, and I have no idea what to do or say. And there are thirty other patients and a dozen students waiting on me.

How in the world do I give comfort?

~ ~ ~

My incapacity in this particular scenario is easy to see, but situations like these abound: a friend is undergoing cancer treatments, a cousin is going through a divorce, another friend loses her job, another's parent just died suddenly from a stroke.

Do we know what to do in those situations? It's easy to be far too confident in ourselves. Victor Hugo wrote,

There is nowhere that the eye of the spirit can find either more splendor or more darkness than in a man. There is nothing more formidable, more complicated, more mysterious, and more infinite. There is a spectacle that is grander than the sea, and it is the sky. There is a spectacle grander than the sky, and it is the interior of the human soul.[3]

To me, this quote captures the necessary posture for thinking about what is going on inside of a human being's soul. It's so easy to be glib, and that is precisely the danger.

If the human soul is a great mystery, then the suffering soul even more so. There is a profound depth inside each of us. Who has suffered and doesn't have a story of some well-intentioned person whose words were wounding, when they were meant to be kind? Marilynne Robinson wrote, "When you're scalded, touch hurts. It makes no difference if it's kindly meant."[4] This is a frightening truth.

How do we bring consolation? Looking to biblical stories for examples of would-be consolers seems to confirm just how difficult it can be. Even Job's friends start out well enough, sitting silently for seven days. However, as soon as they open their mouths, they quickly earn Job's angst, until he says "worthless physicians are you all. Oh that you would keep silent."[5]

When the first son of David and Bathsheba is sick and about to die, everyone around David is worried about how desperate David seems. He won't get up. He won't eat. When the baby dies, they are afraid to tell him, for fear that he will decide to harm himself. Yet he guesses about the child's death before anyone even tells him. Then David gets up, worships, and eats. His servants are surprised by his faith and resilience.[6] Clearly, those who would have comforted him had no idea what was going on inside him.

Later, when David's grown son Absalom dies, David reacts differently. Same guy, but he is in a totally different situation. David weeps openly for his rebellious and conniving son. His display of grief causes a great shame to his army, but at this moment, David is 100 percent father and 0 percent king. It is his general Joab who kicks David into shape, telling him to go out to his men.[7] Joab is effective in helping David, but given that Joab is a bloodthirsty vengeful type (he was the one to kill Absalom contrary to the king's direct order), it's hard to take him for a role model.

Again, we see that the call to console may be clear, but it's not easily done. It's only in Jesus that I find hope. When he arrives at the tomb of his friend Lazarus, he is greeted by Lazarus's two sisters, Martha and Mary.[8] They are in great need of consolation. A little story in Luke 10 gives a glimpse into the differing personalities of these two sisters.[9] Martha is all strength and action, while Mary is all heart and relationship.

When their brother has died and Jesus arrives, they both say the exact same thing to him. "Lord, if you had been here, my brother would not have died." It's half accusation and half question. *Why?* Or more importantly, *Do you really love us?*

Jesus acts and speaks toward each sister in an utterly unique way. There is no formula for consolation, because there is no formula for a human being. To Martha, he speaks of being the resurrection and the life. He speaks to Martha specifically, because he knows her.

With Mary, who had sat at his feet just to be near him, he weeps.

"Weep with those who weep,"[10] says Paul. That's what Jesus does, and that's precisely what I am so hesitant to do. I am a doctor, and I'm not here to weep. I am here to fix the problem that caused the weeping. Yet fundamentally, for so many in need of comfort, the problem will not be fixed. It may heal with time, but that is not the same. For now, things are not okay, and no one can make them okay. So those who suffer have to trust. They have to trust that those who mourn are blessed, because they will, in the end, be comforted.[11] They need to trust the Lord is close to the brokenhearted, and he rescues those who are crushed in spirit.[12] It is a terrible trust that tries to find a little bit of comfort now through hoping that more comfort will be forthcoming in the future, though we don't know when or exactly from where it will come.

Paul Miller talks about the desert that stretches out between our hopes and our reality.[13] This desert is where those who suffer live. If I am called to comfort, then I am called to join them in that desert. If I would weep with them, then I have to open my heart and trust in God for them. I must cling to some hope that God will indeed bring comfort to them. But for the promise of God, there's no automatic guarantee that consolation will come. Maybe the mourning has no end. Maybe the wound will be left gaping. Maybe the whole situation will end in disappointment instead of comfort. This tension calls the sufferer to a profoundly difficult hope and trust. Though admittedly to a much smaller degree, I also have to risk that awful gap between where they are and where they are promised to go.

I don't want to. It's too painful. I have enough of my own problems. It's easier to keep my heart closed. The call to comfort others is a call to maintain hope for those in the most desperate situations, and that means I could just end up with disappointment, dashed hopes, and heartsickness. I resist, saying I can't keep opening my heart every time something goes wrong. There are more tragedies in the world than there are tears to cry for them. This is true. Maybe we can't open our hearts for every person we meet, but our hearts must remain open, at least sometimes. A heart that does not open has no life and no love. Ultimately, we cannot live with hearts that are more bunker than hearth, hearts of stone rather than hearts of flesh.

My choice is between closing up my heart or opening it up to the tempest of my fellow human being's suffering. Each time I really try to comfort, I take the risk to suffer with someone. This is compassion, and it does not come cheaply. I said the call to consolation is clear, but it is not easily done. It may be more true to say that's not cheaply done. A life of compassion comes at a great cost. So maybe I (along with all of the would-be consolers in the biblical accounts I mentioned) seem to lack wisdom or know-how when it comes to consolation, but it's really more a matter of courage and of love.

The call remains: comfort those in affliction. It seems too much for us, but let us not forget the promise. We are not alone, for we give comfort out of the provision of comfort we have received from God. He is the well and the only sufficient source. Sometimes, the costliness of consolation threatens to exhaust our own stores of comfort and leave us dry. But the same God who calls us is there to comfort us, even in our comforting.

Despite my reticence, I do this. From time to time, I weep or otherwise show the truth that I am wrapped up in someone else's suffering, that their sorrow is a sorrow for me as well—not always, or even often. But when I do, there's usually some sign that my presence in their story, brief though it has been, has been a comfort. Either by something they say or even a slightly less strained look on their face, they communicate that the weight of it all is a little lighter for the sharing.

~ ~ ~

Galatians 6:2 tells us to "bear one another's burdens, and so fulfill the law of Christ."

It is a curious thing that we can bear one another's burdens. It seems like it would be impossible. It seems like there's this existential distance between every human soul that cannot be crossed. Though we may sincerely desire to lift part of the burden for someone else, it's simply an unfortunate impossibility. It feels like the load is theirs alone to bear.

The mystery is that experience suggests otherwise. Not every time, but it does seem to happen. How? By the fulfillment of the law, which is, of course, love.[14] Those who truly love, risk, hope, and trust can actually make someone else's burden lighter. It will cost us, for bearing a burden means precisely that one's own journey is made more difficult. In the immortal words of Samwise Gamgee, "Come, Mr. Frodo! I can't carry it for you, but I can carry you."[15] It is never easily done, and we will have to keep walking with others as long as we would bear their burden. But the calling is not in vain, for the one who calls us all is the same God who is the source of all our comfort.

QUESTIONS FOR DISCUSSION AND PERSONAL REFLECTION

1. What does this chapter suggest is the primary promise God offers us when faced with enormous grief and a call to bring comfort? Do you agree, or do you have another way to articulate what God promises?

2. Describe a time when you wanted to comfort someone in grief, but you felt unable to do so. What made that particular situation difficult?

3. Describe a time when you have personally suffered. What did people say to comfort you? What was helpful and what was unhelpful or hurtful?

4. What is the connection between our capacity to have hope for someone who grieves and our ability to comfort them?

5. How might you try to bring comfort to someone without opening up your own heart? Why might we have this reflex? What difference does it make?

13

Resurrection

Be still. A man who seems to be
A gardener rises out of the ground,
Stands like a tree, shakes off the dark,
The bluebells opening at his feet,
The light a figured cloth of song.

—WENDELL BERRY[1]

❧

One day in the NICU, a young Kenyan woman brings her baby girl in, and the nurse asks me to evaluate her. Her name is Cherotich (a tribal name meaning "baby girl born at the time of day that the cows come home"). They are just outside the door, sitting on a white, painted bench. The young woman unwraps her baby for me. I squat down and pull out my stethoscope. I examine her lungs, head, reflexes, and hydration. She is weak to the point of minimal movement. Both the soft spot on her head and her eyes are sunken. She is obviously sick.

Cherotich is three weeks old, and yesterday, she started having fevers. Then today, she stopped eating. I ask the woman if everything was all right when she delivered the baby. She has a small, embarrassed smile as she glances off somewhere down the hallway. She is not the mother, she says. The baby's mother died the day after delivering this little girl. She had some kind of bad infection. However, the baby was fine, and the family took her home. This young woman is the mom's younger sister, unmarried with no kids of her own.

Given all of this, it is not surprising that Cherotich is sick. Infants in poor countries without a mother often don't survive. They lack an appropriate source of nutrition, and whatever they do get as an alternative is difficult to give in a way that is clean and nourishing enough for a newborn. In addition, they are missing out on the antibodies normally present in a mom's breast milk, and in this infection-laden environment, that omission is a very big deal.

We admit Cherotich to the neonatal unit, and once her initial treatment is underway, I come back and examine her more thoroughly, noticing this time her legs are really stiff. With my hand, I try and bend her leg at the knee, but it is strangely difficult. It's possible this is due to meningitis or maybe an electrolyte imbalance, but our tests will eventually show that these things are not the cause. Unfortunately, I've seen this before, and it's an ominous sign. All the babies that have come in with a similar stiffness have died. It's reminiscent of *rigor mortis*, only it happens before death. It seems to be a sign of an inevitable end.

My expectations are low. However, the next day, Cherotich is still alive, and the fevers have lessened. She still can't take any milk by mouth, but she is tolerating what we put down the tube that goes from her nose to her stomach. Her legs are still stiff, but she appears a little less dehydrated and has managed to urinate a couple of times.

Over the next few days, Cherotich stabilizes. The fevers go away, she becomes more active, and she is able to drink formula from a cup. After seven days, we are able to stop her antibiotics, and after about ten days, her legs relax and move with a normal amount of tone. Then, she goes home. It is a testament to the simple power of ordinary things and the endurance of those who implement them.

A few weeks later, one of the medical staff calls me over to the clinic to see another child. After evaluating the child, he tells me there's also a lady outside who wants to see me. I exit the room, and there on the waiting bench is Cherotich's aunt. She unwraps the blanket in her lap, and there is Cherotich. Well and healthy, she has come back just to be weighed and vaccinated. She is lying on a blue and white blanket, and to commemorate her visit to the clinic, she is decked out in a secondhand (or third or fourth) peach dress with frilly sleeves. It's probably sized for a nine-month-old, but what it lacks in fit, it makes up for in sequins and whorls and generally superfluous bling. She is sleeping, and her aunt is smiling. And so am I.

Cherotich's recovery reminds me of resurrection. She didn't die, but I thought she was going to. My impression is that her family also feared as much. I didn't expect she would leave the hospital alive, much less that I would get to see her thriving several weeks later.

~ ~ ~

It happened again around the same time. I step into the emergency room to see if I can offer any help in the few minutes before rounds start, and I notice some commotion in the corner. Several nurses and a doctor are surrounding a small body on a stretcher, and one nurse is pushing air into the lungs of the child with a respiratory bag and mask.

The child's name is Chepngetich (meaning "baby girl born at the time of day when the cows go out"), and though she is fifteen months old, she only weighs about seven pounds. She is literally skin over skeleton. Her eyes are sunken, and her bones stick out. She came in gasping her final breaths. The ER team saw her and started bagging her in order to push air into her exhausted lungs.

It seems Chepngetich is already gone. We are breathing for her, and her severe malnutrition means her body has all but shut down. Her heart is barely pumping, her body temperature is unregulated, and she is susceptible to the slightest infection.

We have medicines and special nutritional milk to feed her, but kids like this don't survive long enough to benefit from them. Despite all our efforts, something will go wrong—and soon. She will stop breathing, or her sugar will drop, or she will vomit up some milk and block her airway. If she makes it to the early hours of the morning, when the temperature drops, she will pass away silently in the chilly night.

Faithful hands go to their faithful work. God's grace is alive in the ordinary and the mundane. Someone starts an IV. From somewhere, an oversized wooden light box appears to serve as an incubator. Someone else puts a tube down her nose to start delivering cautious nutrition.

The next day, Chepngetich is still alive, lying in the light box, but basically comatose. We pray, and discuss, and continue to treat. Four days later, she can sip from a cup if someone holds her head up, so the tube comes out. Two weeks later, she has gained two pounds and can sit up in bed. The whole pediatrics team can't believe it. It's like life from the dead. Then, we send her home.

~ ~ ~

In Hebrews 11, the author talks about Abraham offering up his son, Isaac, as a sacrifice, noting, "he considered that God was able even to raise him from the dead, from which, figuratively speaking, he did receive him back."[2] Isaac didn't die either, but there was this same feeling of resurrection. In Abraham's mind, he had already let Isaac go. He was lost. Yet Abraham received his son back, as if from the dead.

When I reflect on it, it seems that this type of resurrection happens more often than I usually realize. I have had numerous discussions with families of very sick patients, wanting to warn them that things look grim (and often thinking that they look even grimmer). Then, against my expectations, the family receives back their father, their daughter, their baby. Emmanuel was like that. Alice was like that. Chepngetich and Cherotich were like that. It's possible that, as the doctor, it makes me look a little foolish, but no one has ever stopped to take note of it. They have too much joy.

The resurrection of Jesus is the cornerstone of the Christian faith. It's the hinge upon which the world turns. Jesus passed from death to life and so do his followers. N. T. Wright says we under-celebrate resurrection.[3] He proposes that, since the forty days before Easter are traditionally given to focusing on the suffering and loss of Christ (i.e., Lent), perhaps the forty days after Easter should be spent celebrating the resurrection of Christ—a time to acknowledge the new life we see in the world around us, a time to take on new things and bring them to life.

Can we do that in such a world as ours? If we look the question straight in the eye, we are forced to remember that, though Chepngetich is still alive, she has the same poverty-stricken situation at meal times, and the same health threats will loom large for many months. Though Cherotich is still alive, she probably wouldn't have gotten sick but for the death of her mother. And her mother did not come back.

This brings us, of course, to the very center of the promise of resurrection. A promise given that we "may not grieve as others do who have no hope."[4] Resurrection is the grand eucatastrophe. The grand rewriting of the ending. There is hope now for Cherotich's mother. There is hope for Mercy and Dieudonné and Claudette and all the others I have mentioned. There is hope for all of us.

I grew up in a cultural moment where Christians minimized the significance of the resurrection. We understood that the substitutionary death of Jesus brought us forgiveness of sins, but we weren't quite sure what his resurrection from the dead added to the story. It was as if a Christian faith founded primarily on the resurrection was lacking in real-world application. We preferred to emphasize how God can change our lives here and now. If our faith can transform our relationships, our marriage, our self-image, or our mood—well, that's a faith that matters. That has real merit. Resurrection was fine but insufficient and kind of irrelevant.

The fallacy is obvious. The reality is there's nothing more universally applicable to all people in all places in every era of history than the resurrection. Death can be ignored but not avoided. We are all staring at a big question mark, and it's to this question, even to this fear, that the promise of resurrection is offered. It's inextricably rooted in Jesus who says, "I am the resurrection and the life. Whoever believes in me, though he die, yet shall he live, and everyone who lives and believes in me shall never die."[5] Then he sets those words into action. Jesus dies and rises again, the firstfruits and the grand foretaste of what is promised.

Make no mistake. Death may be a part of life, in the sense that it happens to everyone, but it's not part of life in the same way as birth, childhood, family, and parenthood. Death may be a part of life for now, but that's because life is broken, and it has yet to be fully renewed. Death is the enemy to be defeated. "The last enemy to be destroyed is death."[6]

Yet, in a strangely redemptive mystery, death, like suffering, has become sacred ground because God has now walked there as well. And now, when we come to death, we go where our Savior has gone before us, and we hear his voice calling us beyond it—to resurrection.

Maybe we so rarely think on it because it is too much for us. "Such knowledge is too wonderful for me."[7] Too wonderful for the burdens in my heart and the suffering of the world around me, but the promise persists. The promise will not be silent. It echoes off the walls of the canyon of this world in every small taste of resurrected life. Abraham heard it when Isaac was given back into his arms. I saw it in the smile of Cherotich's aunt, who lost a sister but holds her daughter still. Paul speaks of that promise:

> Listen, I tell you a mystery: We will not all sleep, but we
> will all be changed—in a flash, in the twinkling of an eye,
> at the last trumpet. For the trumpet will sound, the dead

will be raised imperishable, and we will be changed. For the perishable must clothe itself with the imperishable, and the mortal with immortality. When the perishable has been clothed with the imperishable, and the mortal with immortality, then the saying that is written will come true: "Death has been swallowed up in victory."[8]

We have surely borne the image of the man of dust, and just so, God promises we will just as surely bear the image of the man of heaven—Jesus in his glorious resurrection life.[9]

My conviction is that, as this hope of future resurrection shapes us, it will spread. It will permeate the present world around us with its life-giving promise. Thus the false dichotomy of hope for the present world and hope for the future world rightly dissolves, for the same one is transforming all things with his single living hope.

Let us celebrate the hope that is ours. Let us celebrate it for forty days and beyond. Let us celebrate in the face of death and tragedy. Let us celebrate it until Chepngetich and Cherotich and her mom and all the cows come home together. Let us remember the promise, and so, though we grieve, let us grieve with hope.

QUESTIONS FOR DISCUSSION AND
PERSONAL REFLECTION

1. How do you interact with the Christian promise of resur-
    rection after death? How has your particular church culture
    treated the resurrection? Is it overemphasized or minimized
    because of a lack of real-world application?
2. Describe a time when you glimpsed resurrection, i.e., when
    new life surprised you from a situation that seemed all but
    dead.
3. What does the resurrection of Christ have to say about life
    prior to death? How do we live or practice resurrection now?
4. Imagine the death of the last person who will die—the final
    moment before God's promises are all fulfilled and death
    dies. Imagine knowing that death is no more. How does the
    promise of such a reality give us hope for now?
5. Where do you overlook resurrection in your own life and
    the lives around you? How can you celebrate them more and
    cultivate the praise and gratitude for which they call?

14

Darkness and Light

A heart's-clarion!
Away grief's gasping, joyless days, dejection.
Across my foundering deck shone
A beacon, an eternal beam
—GERARD MANLEY HOPKINS[1]

~

Mass suicide is what is written on the chart.

What does *that* mean? I wonder as I flip through the few pages on the clipboard next to the bed of a six-year-old boy in the ICU. There's not a lot of information in the chart, so I ask the doctor who had been on call last night.

It started with a young woman drinking a pesticide in an attempt to commit suicide. Such pesticides are readily available in the Kenyan agricultural setting, and if people drink enough, their hearts will slow down, their level of consciousness will decrease, and they will slowly stop breathing. If people drink the particularly bad kind, their lungs will also fill up with fluid. At our hospital, we unfortunately see these cases pretty much every day. The suicide rate in this part of Kenya isn't necessarily higher; the pesticide is simply the most available means. Some family member or friend or bystander brings in those who have drunk the pesticide, and often we can save them. It's grisly work, for sure, but not out of the ordinary for the hospital staff.

The difference in this case is that, along with this young woman drinking the poison, she also gave it to her three sons. I don't know whether she forced it down their fighting throats, or whether they calmly and trustingly took the foul-smelling cup their mother gave them. Either way, they took it.

The youngest of them, who was three years old, died during the night, shortly after arriving at the hospital. The six-year-old stopped breathing, and so the overnight team put him on a mechanical ventilator. The eight-year-old is semiconscious in the next bed with a face mask blowing oxygen. He is far from stable, and we're hoping to avoid having to put him on a ventilator as well. At the end of the small room is the woman herself. It would appear she gave herself the same dose as her children, because she is awake and breathing normally, which would be expected due to her larger size.

It's a horror. I cannot fathom what would push a mother to try and kill not only herself but also her three sons. Maybe she has long endured a state of major depression, and then something happened to push her over the edge, like a husband who ran away with another woman. Maybe her family decided to disown her, and she didn't know where she would live or how she would eat. Maybe someone threatened to kill her and her sons. I have no idea, but one thing is sure. Whatever the cause, it was horror as well.

Now, she's alive, and she's aware she killed her youngest son. She is in the same room as the others, and she has only to turn her head to see how close she has brought them to the brink of dying.

It is the worst thing I have ever seen.

~ ~ ~

The everyday events of my work have an undeniable tone of sadness. Tragedy is the predominant image. But in this case, we very clearly see something else that is usually more hazy but always lurking. There is evil in the sadness, some sense that things didn't have to be this way. Things could have been different. They should have been different. I don't always have the strength to look directly at the evil, but it's always there.

I want to write this story, the worst case I have ever seen, and then still say this: since moving to Africa, I have never been so acutely aware of the positive presence of the goodness of God in the world. I know that is jarring, but that's the point. It jars me. I'm not sure what caused this increased awareness. Perhaps it's God's particular grace to help me endure, or perhaps it's a simple matter of striking contrasts. At any rate, this goodness, which may be shattered and mixed like one would expect in our fallen world, is still emphatically and jarringly present.

One day, a couple months after the mass suicide attempt (where the other two boys did, in the end, survive), I am walking from the NICU to the pediatrics ward. To get there, I exit a door and walk on a kind of balcony between the buildings for about thirty feet. There's a right turn on the balcony, and at the bend, I can look left out over the hills. They are the striking shades of green that tea fields variously take on as they mature. The green goes up and up, stitched together like a quilt, all the way to the bald peak of Motigo Hill, where sheep are grazing under the blue sky. The air is fresh, and there's a slight breeze.

Standing there, leaning on the rail is a physician assistant student, a young man visiting from Kentucky. He is looking out at the hills, and I can see tears on his cheeks. He looks briefly at me, and then turns back to the view.

"I just saw my first child born here," he says.

Uh-oh. My mind immediately goes to a dozen awful things that could have gone wrong. I remember that this guy is very early in his education, and I don't like the idea that some tragic birth would be his first impression of obstetrics.

"How did it go?" I ask quietly.

He continues to stare at the horizon. "Hmm?" he says, as if he has already forgotten that I'm there. "Oh, it went fine. Just fine. It's just amazing, you know?"

∼ ∼ ∼

For all the sadness, if you walked through our hospital, the predominant sound is not wailing. It's laughter and the chatting of friends—and not just from the families whose loved one is getting better, but from the others as well. A baby snuggles up to her mom. A gentle wind brushes my face. An ibis calls as it flies overhead. There are red blossoms in the treetops. The chai cup warms my cold hands. A friend is only too glad to help. Two kids play together outside, running and laughing for no particular reason.

It is goodness, and it is everywhere. For this story of mass suicide, I don't know where the light is. Maybe there isn't any. Nevertheless, I do maintain that the goodness of the world in which that woman lived was abundant, though I have no doubt she was unable to see it. At the very least, she had three sons, each of whose birth was enough to bring tears to the eyes of a grown foreigner.

Buechner writes, "What's lost is nothing to what's found, and all the death that ever was, set next to life, would scarcely fill a cup."[2] And he's right.

Philosophers talk about the problem of evil. I'm no philosopher, but I understand the question like this: If God is all-good and all-powerful, then why is there evil in the world? Perhaps God is not good or not powerful. Or maybe he's not even there. Anyone who has seriously tried to engage the darkness has felt this tension. These questions have troubled us all, at least some of the time.

There are arguments and counter-arguments. They very well might be worth engaging. I only want to add one piece to the discussion, something that maybe people overlook. Yes, there is great evil in the world, but there is also all this goodness in the world. It's everywhere, and it's palpably real. If God isn't there or he isn't good, then where did all the goodness come from? Its presence also cries out for explanation. If we would speak of the "problem of evil," could we also speak of a philosophical "problem of good"?

~ ~ ~

Stanley Hauerwas says the philosophical problem of evil didn't really bother Christians for most of their history. He says it became prominent during the Enlightenment, when God became defined principally by abstract concepts such as omnipotence, omniscience, and omnipresence. This is in contrast to defining God primarily by the stories of his relationship with his people. The presence of evil became difficult to reconcile with this abstract concept of God. However, for the generations of people whose God was not abstract, but rather a particular God with a particular character and history, this question didn't ever seem to cause much anguish.

What did Christians do, in the face of evil, for the first sixteen or so centuries of Christianity? Hauerwas says, "Historically, Christians provided not a 'solution' to the problem of evil, but a community of care that made suffering possible to absorb."[3] This certainly has implications for the call to console those who suffer, but I think it also says something about the problem of good and evil.

Maybe it's another way of saying the same thing. Maybe this community of care that makes suffering possible to absorb is, in fact, the emphatic presence of God's goodness. When we tap into it, we understand how powerful and pervasive God's goodness really is. After all, Jesus does refer to us, the community of those who follow him, as "the light of the world."[4] It's remarkably the same words he uses elsewhere to describe himself.[5] In this community, we see the good hand of God in the world and in our lives. In the face of evil, we encounter, all around us, the goodness of God. In the face of the darkness, we encounter the light. The light is strong. It shines in the dark, and it overcomes. So we can endure, even with joy.

~ ~ ~

I previously described goodness as pinpricks of light on a dark curtain, places where the light gets through, betraying that, back there somewhere, a world of unbreakable, undiminished radiance is shining. To me, that image conveys how I often see the world. But I wonder whether it's not truer to say the darkness and light are closer to being reversed. Maybe the goodness is the rule, like a banner of golden, solid light that's contaminated here and there with specks of darkness, little unnatural pollutants that don't belong.

Evil is a problem. There is an unnaturalness about it. People know it doesn't belong. Despite the tortuous and self-deceiving nature of the human heart, human beings are not content as long as any darkness remains. It may be only a speck of darkness, but we want it gone, and rightly so. Evil was not part of God's intention for his creation. Thus, for all its ubiquity, it's not supposed to be there. God also wants it gone, and Christians are called to reflect him in our role as the light of the world by working to eliminate this darkness. Yet for now, it remains.

In the face of darkness, we can look forward. We hope, for a promise is given to us that all things are being restored—all things. That unnatural darkness, great or small, will be utterly banished, purged with a brilliant light that's whiter than snow.

In the meantime, while we wait for that final restoration, what do we do? The calling of Jesus is clear: the body of Christ is to be the community that makes it possible to absorb the suffering. We are to bear the tears and the laughter, both of which can celebrate the goodness of God in the world even now. We are to be the light of the world, overcoming the darkness.

QUESTIONS FOR DISCUSSION AND
PERSONAL REFLECTION

1. What does this chapter suggest is the primary promise God offers us when faced with the enormity of the world's darkness, even its evil? Do you agree, or do you have another way to articulate what God promises?

2. Describe the worst darkness you have seen.

3. In your daily life and work, where do you routinely overlook God's goodness?

4. How can we, as a community, be the light of the world?

5. How can we, as a community, show forth the light of the world which is Jesus?

15

Redemption

Oh the height and depth of mercy!
Oh the length and breadth of love!
Of the fullness of redemption!
Pledge of endless life above!

—FANNY CROSBY[1]

Darlène is seven years old and slipped into a coma this morning. Her mom says she was healthy until yesterday. She started having some fevers, and then this morning, she just didn't wake up. Her back is arched, and her whole body is rigid. Her eyes are half open, and she is drooling.

Most kids here in Burundi with the combination of a coma and a fever have cerebral malaria, and though Darlène's malaria test is negative, given the severity of her condition, the hospital staff and I start her on aggressive antimalarial therapy. Less frequently, but still fairly commonly, we see bacterial meningitis cause a similar picture, so we start that treatment as well. She worries me, but a lot of these kids will turn around within a few days—but not Darlène.

The next day, her fever is still high, and nothing has changed. After three days, red blistery lesions appear around her mouth. Now we have another diagnosis to consider, because rarely, herpes (including the run-of-the-mill kind that causes cold sores) can cause an infection in the brain.

Herpes encephalitis has a treatment. It's old, cheap, safe, and effective, so much so that it's often replaced in wealthier countries with a newer version that's more expensive and just a bit easier to use. But, just at present, we don't have this treatment. We don't have the IV form recommended for encephalitis. We don't even have the pill form. We have nothing. So, we're just waiting it out, giving her IV fluids and oxygen.

On her sixth day in the hospital, I notice one of her pupils is notably larger than the other. Neither one of them constrict appropriately when I shine my flashlight in her eyes. This is basically a sign of impending brain death. It's hard to be sicker than this and still be alive.

Darlène's mom knows she isn't getting better. She's tired and understandably overwhelmed. She says she wants to take Darlène home. "To pray," she says, and I think that means "to die," but it's not my place to say what she means. I tell her we are already praying for her, that God is here, and we will continue to pray for her. I tell her I know Darlène isn't doing well, but I don't think it would even be possible to transport Darlène home in her current condition.

She assents and asks me to pray. I sit beside her, with the great white coat cloud of witnesses all around, and we pray for her.

The next day, Darlène is still alive. The day after that, she is doing just a bit better. Mom is satisfied. Each day, she does just a little bit better. Her breathing eases. She is able to swallow some food. I am shocked. Her mom never lets me leave the bedside without praying for her daughter. About a week after noticing her unequal pupils, we send Darlène home.

Her pupil is still big. She can only sit up with great assistance. She smiles a bit at me, but she doesn't talk. There is a good chance she will stay this way. But who knows? If we keep praying, what could be gained?

I don't know what she was like before she got sick. Yet it seems she was a healthy Burundian seven-year-old girl. She was in her first few years of school, and it's easy to picture her walking over the red dirt hills with her friends, laughing at one another's jokes. When I compare that image to the girl I know now, it's hard.

She's alive, and I thought she would die. But she still needs so much healing.

This is how it is a lot of the time. Even though healing has come, there is a great ache at its incompleteness.

~ ~ ~

There is a short phrase in the chorus of an old Fanny Crosby hymn, "Oh, the fullness of redemption!"[2] I don't know the tune. I first heard the phrase a few years ago while visiting the church where I grew up in Nashville. A young woman was singing on stage with tattered jeans, bare feet, and an incredible mop of unruly brown curls. She was singing her own arrangement of the hymn. It was all minor chords and acoustic guitar resonance. She was strumming her heart out, up on her toes for emphasis, drawing out the word *fullness*. It was music to match the lyric. She was crying out.

My heart is usually crying out for the same thing. Darlène's story has a lot of redemption in it, and I'm thankful for that. But it's not "fullness of redemption"—not by a long shot. My heart yearns for fullness of redemption, but most of the time, life falls way short.

The malnourished kid gets over the pneumonia, but the family still doesn't have enough food. The broken femur is put back together, but the roads are just as dangerous as ever. Two friends are reconciled after a bitter argument, but a slight, shadowy fear never completely goes away, so it flares up every now and then in heated moments. Healing is incomplete, and reconciliation is imperfect.

But there remains a promise. Jesus says, "Behold, I am making all things new."[3] Jesus promises fullness, completion, even perfection, though I often have no idea what that looks like. It might be hard to imagine, but it is beautiful nonetheless.

~ ~ ~

I see something of this tension in a wonderfully strange story in the gospel of Mark.[4] Mark, who normally zooms from plot to plot, slows down and tells a strangely poignant and very human story. Jesus gets off the boat in the country of the Gerasenes, and a demon-possessed man meets him. The backstory is that, for a long time, everyone had tried to shackle and subdue this man, but they had failed. He lives alone among the tombs.

Face to face with Jesus, his demons realize they are beaten, and Jesus commands them to go. In a notably strange twist, the demons negotiate, and the result is that Jesus sends them into a herd of two thousand pigs, which then run off a cliff to their deaths. I guess this is meant to show just how many demons there were in this guy, but it reveals more than that by the people's subsequent reaction.

People come from the surrounding area and see two things: A long-tormented man now at peace and in his right mind and an amazingly scary financial loss in the form of dead livestock. They plead for Jesus to go.

Here's the poignant part: the formerly demon-possessed man begs to go with Jesus. He was in the dark for so long, and he has just rediscovered the light in Jesus. He wants to get in the boat and go with Jesus.

Jesus's response is heartbreaking. "Go home to your friends and tell them how much the Lord has done for you."[5]

I can see the disappointment and disbelief on his face. I can hear the thoughts running through his head: *What home? What friends? These are the same people who tried to chain me up for years! Are they going to forget that fear overnight? These are the same people who valued their pigs more than my healing! Jesus, you are the only light I have seen. You are the only friend I have. Why can't I come with you?*

Traditional cultures like Burundi often have amazingly strong family commitments. However, when I have asked Burundian friends if they would take a family member like this demon-possessed man back into their home, they were far from certain. Even in the best-case scenario, it's hard to imagine there wasn't always a shadow of suspicion in those relationships. The story goes on to tell that the man went throughout the Decapolis telling what Jesus had done. The Decapolis wasn't a single place, but an area of ten cities. I picture him wandering around because of a certain misfit feeling that never quite went away.

He received so much healing, but I bet he was still yearning for fullness of redemption.

∼ ∼ ∼

Sometimes I get a glimpse of this fullness. I remember my wife Rachel's patient Mary, who had been pregnant ten times and had no living children. They had all been miscarriages or the babies had died shortly after birth. She suffered pain and infirmity in her body but also shame and shattered dreams. She came to Rachel halfway through this tenth pregnancy, desperate for help. Rachel treated her for weeks until one morning, things went bad and the baby's heartbeat disappeared. She was rushed to a C-section and delivered a limp, non-breathing baby.

However, with our ordinary but immediate intervention, the baby perked up and started breathing. He was still very premature and was sent to the NICU. Mary stayed with him there for thirty days as he first stabilized and then grew. She would have gladly stayed six months. At the end of it, she took her baby home. In another story reminiscent of this one, Sarah named her baby Laughter.[6] It's the best kind of laughter, and it echoes still through Mary's story. However, Mary named her baby Gift.

Mary had a physical problem, but she also had social shame, marital distress, years of dashed expectations, and who knows what else. Rachel and I didn't do anything heroic, but all the lines of the story had been woven together in such a way that our simple work brought about so much healing in so many ways. Yet even such, a story doesn't erase the shadow of all her other losses. It's a glimpse of the fullness of redemption, but just a glimpse.

∼ ∼ ∼

I remember Fidès, who started going blind from cataracts in her thirties. At that time in Burundi, only one person was operating on eye disease, and she had no access to treatment for this simple problem. My ophthalmologist teammate John says that life expectancy in Africa when you go blind is only five years.

She told John about how she and her husband kept her problem a secret, because people would expect him to leave her or take another wife. Then, she became pregnant, even as her vision was deteriorating. By the time of the birth of her daughter, she couldn't see her daughter's face. She would try and make faces to make her baby smile, but she didn't know if it was working.

Then, her neighbor told her John had opened an eye clinic in her region. She came and got her cataracts fixed. He took her bandages off the next day, and she saw her daughter for the first time. She was beautiful.

Like Mary, Fidès had a physical problem, and because of it, she also had a tragically low life expectancy. But she also had great social shame, resulting in an inability to live honestly with her neighbors. She was incredibly alone and isolated. Her roles as a mother and a wife were being severely challenged by her disease. Once again, everything aligned, and a simple intervention brought so much healing on so many levels. Here is *almost* fullness of redemption, more of a foretaste to make me imagine what could be waiting for all of us. As good as this is, Jesus promises us something more.

~ ~ ~

When Jesus says, "I am making all things new," he is talking about souls, but not just souls. He is not just talking about bodies, either, but everything: hearts, relationships, families, communities, knowledge, the earth, and all the material world. All of creation groans while it waits for freedom from its bondage to decay and for the glory of the children of God.[7] The new heavens will meet the new earth.[8] The Tree of Life will never cease to yield its fruit, and its leaves will be for the healing of the nations.[9] That is fullness of redemption. The brokenness runs deep. Deeper still runs the redemption that Christ has wrought and that he is even now accomplishing. Far as the curse is found, no dark corner will be left where the light of Christ does not shine.

The word *redemption*, however, is a bit odd. It has a formal definition, but it also seems to mean something in my imagination that surpasses that definition. In its common usage, "to redeem" means "to buy back."[10] Thus people redeem gift cards and credit card points. They buy them back. In this same way, God buys his people back. He redeems us, and we are now his.

Yet redemption brings much more to mind. The connotation of the word is something more intricate. It signifies newness, a righting of wrongs, a eucatastrophe where all the sin and darkness and brokenness are somehow transfigured into something amazingly beautiful. Redemption, in this sense, makes everything even better than if it had never been broken in the first place. *That* is the redemption whose fullness we are yearning for.

Why does this seemingly simple word, redemption, which means "to buy back," stir up all these dreams? Redemption's meaning runs so deeply precisely because God is doing the buying. He buys us and our fractured lives out of darkness and into his marvelous light. Now we are his. We belong to the one who dreamed up Eden in the first place. We belong to the one who took the fallenness of mankind, and through his own suffering and self-sacrifice, wrought something better even than what we had lost. We belong to the one who is always with us and who is making all things new. We belong to the Maker and Keeper of Promises. We belong to the one who is the utter source of all the splendor, grace, and love that has ever been. God is buying back his entire glorious design for his world.

Our lives have been bought back by this God, and now reunited with him, we do well to have every expectation that the promise of the fullness of redemption will be everything we dream it might be.

The next line in the Crosby hymn is, "Take the world, but give me Jesus."[11] When I hold this image of the fullness of redemption in my mind, I can sing this line with all my heart. Take the world—not because it isn't lovely, not because, even in its fallenness, there isn't something of splendor in every drop of every morning, not because there isn't joy and glory and beauty. There is, but give me Jesus, for he is holding out something infinitely more.

QUESTIONS FOR DISCUSSION AND
PERSONAL REFLECTION

1. What does this chapter suggest is the primary promise
   God offers us when faced with the persistent brokenness of
   life despite all our efforts and all the partial solutions they
   may produce? Do you agree, or do you have another way to
   articulate what God promises?

2. Describe a time when, even though there has been partial
   redemption or resolution, you (or someone else) were still
   grieving for the persistent brokenness, for the lack of fullness of redemption.

3. Describe a circumstance that is the closest you have ever
   experienced to "fullness of redemption," either in your life
   or someone you know. What was it like to confront that situation? What brought this redemption about? Was it extraordinary effort, everyday faithfulness in small things, seeming
   chance, or some combination?

4. What images are called to mind by the word *redemption*?
   How would you explain the full sense of what redemption
   entails to someone who is not a Christian?

Epilogue:
Promises in the Dark

Let us not grow weary in doing good.
—GALATIANS 6:9

How shall we sing the LORD's song in a foreign land?
—PSALM 137:4

❧

I have a hard time relating to John the Baptist. He seems so strong, even brash, bucking societal norms and calling the power players a "brood of vipers"[1] to their faces. He seems so sure of his vocation. John knows he's preparing the way for the Messiah, and sure enough, he recognizes Jesus when he comes.

In many ways, my life seems so contrary to John's. I'm surrounded by situations I can't handle and mysteries I don't understand. I might look for salvation from those in power only to turn around and miss Jesus when he comes to me in an unexpected place that probably shouldn't have been so unexpected.

But then John the Baptist is thrown in prison. Now, I can relate to John in prison.[2] This man, who seemed so strong, sends his disciples to Jesus to ask, "Are you the one who is to come or shall we look for another?" Whatever he expected when he baptized Jesus, John decides it doesn't match up well enough with the reality that surrounds him.

The question is burning inside him, and John has to release it. *Jesus, is the kingdom of God really coming? Is it really near? Everything still seems just as incredibly broken and tattered and unredeemed as ever. This world still seems to be inexorably heading toward death, not life. Jesus, now that you're here, aren't you going to reconcile all things to yourself? I can understand that I won't be able to see your final, perfected work right now, but this hardly feels like new creation at all. I know I've felt, seen, and even proclaimed this in the past, but it's just terribly hard to believe right now.*

When the message of John's doubts arrives, Jesus heals sicknesses and disabilities, and he chases out demons. Jesus tells John's disciples to go back and report what they have seen: The blind see. The lame walk. Lepers are cleansed. The deaf hear. The dead are raised. The poor hear the good news. Blessed is the one who is not offended by me.[3]

How did John receive this answer? We don't know. It seems to be Jesus's way of saying, "No, John, you're not wrong. Witness the evidence that God's kingdom indeed comes in my wake." Did John understand? Was he encouraged? Was he able to trust more in God's promises in the days that followed? We don't know. John's circumstances did not change for the better. He was executed before ever getting released.

Jesus seems to be saying, "John, trust me. Have faith. All things are not yet made new, but there are signs. There are inbreakings. There are firstfruits, seals, down payments, promises

of a bigger thing to come. Hang in there, John!" Was John able to
do that? Are we?

The funny thing is that where I live, every day is arguably
quite similar to Jesus's testimony. In the hospital where I work,
because of God's kingdom, the blind see, the lame walk, and
people with terrible medical conditions (including the occasional
leper) are healed. Those who were all but dead are seemingly resurrected, and the poor hear the good news. It's easy to imagine
visitors to our hospital receiving the type of encouragement that
it seems Jesus is wanting to give John. "I see the signs!" they say.
"It's for real!"

But daily life inside the hospital feels different. I see the rest
as well. I see the young people who are dying. I see the lame man
who had a stroke and is likely to remain lame, go home, develop
bedsores, and die. I see the blindness from meningitis that won't
heal. I see beautiful people who suffer and die because they are
poor in a poor country. I see dysfunctional systems and fractured relationships. I see misplaced hope leading to depression. I
see broken connections to ourselves, to each other, to our work,
and to the earth. The signs that point to Jesus's kingdom don't
feel like enough.

"Blessed is the one who is not offended by me," Jesus concludes his message to John. It's as if Jesus knows how difficult it is
to keep trusting, "Look, what I'm about to say is hard. But don't
get offended. Hear me out. Don't close your heart at these tough
words. Hang in there."

～ ～ ～

"What is God doing?" we ask when sorrow overwhelms us. "How
could God be present in the midst of all this?" we wonder when

our failures seem so pointless. We are called to hope in the promises of God while our feet still pound the dust of a world full of brokenness. The psalmist cries out, "How shall we sing the LORD's song in a foreign land?"[4] The implication is that these songs belong to God's land, while we are exiled in some other forsaken place. So, God, do not ask us to sing *those* songs in *this* land. Do not ask us to hope in those promises in the midst of this world. What we need is evidence that in some mysteriously unshakeable way, this land is still the Lord's land. His arm is not too short to save, and he is always working.[5] We need to remember the promises are true. But how?

How do we persevere in a world such as ours, fraught with such perils as it is? Moreover, how do we walk with those in need? The sorrow and darkness can crash down on us like the unrelentingly pounding surf. The urge to flee toward safety and shelter is overwhelming. We may feel that just surviving would be more than good enough, and yet Jesus calls us to more, to enter into the hurt and into the darkness of others. This is undeniably what Jesus did, and we are called to follow him.

Yet we are so afraid. We are afraid we do not have the strength or the courage. We are afraid that the toll on our hearts will be too much. We are afraid either burnout or cynicism is inevitable. We have felt these threats, or we might be so afraid of facing the threats that we never venture out in the first place.

There is a struggle in our hearts. Because of this, logistical or technical solutions may offer some help, but they will not win the day on their own merits. We are looking for a heart solution.

Maybe that's why we are so afraid. We know the darkness is not only out there, but it is in here as well. Our hearts are divided.

They are dappled like the forest floor, with some parts in the sun and other parts in the shadow. Solzhenitsyn's famous saying still rings true, "The line dividing good and evil cuts through the heart of every human being."[6] We are people of sorrow and people of joy. We build, and we tear down. We believe, and we doubt. We love but so incompletely. We do not do as we want to do. We are like the Old Testament Israelites, running back and forth between our God of endless grace and truth and ignoble little idols of soot. How can such a heart survive in such a world as this?

The promises of God are given to sustain us on this road. They are not ethereal abstractions, but rather promises as real and everyday as the dust of the path we walk. Though it's never easy, we find, along the way, the reminders and the whispers that the promises are true and that the one who promises is faithful. He has placed these promises in the dark, precisely where he knows we need them. They shine in the night sky like eternal diamonds, like Abraham's descendants, more numerous than the sands on an obsidian shore.

We must return again and again to God's promises. We must write them on our doorposts and speak them to one another as we walk along the roads of our world. We must sing them together and let them direct our dreams.

All things are being made new. The light shines in the darkness, and the darkness has not overcome it. God is greater than our hearts. He has conquered the world. He knows us better than we do ourselves, and he has loved us unconditionally. There is nothing left to fear.

"So we do not lose heart. Though our outer self is wasting away, our inner self is being renewed day by day."[7]

QUESTIONS FOR DISCUSSION AND
PERSONAL REFLECTION

1. What are the signs of God's kingdom come that you see in your life? How do these signs encourage you? How are you discouraged despite them?

2. Where does your heart struggle to believe God's promises? Which promises are difficult to really trust and why?

3. What does your heart seek more than God's kingdom, thus causing you to minimize the significance of God's promises? Common alternatives include praise or admiration from other people, knowledge that a certain goal has been accomplished, or a degree of personal comfort.

4. Consider selecting one to three of the promises articulated in these chapters (preferably in scriptural form) and memorizing them in an effort to work them into your heart.

The next time you fail to prioritize God's kingdom (or fail your intention to memorize the promises chosen in question #4), remember the promise of God's great, unmerited love.

Acknowledgments

~

It is a humbling joy to see how many wonderful people have given of their time and talent to leave their mark on this book. Alyssa Pfister, Brian Beise, Steve Telian, and Paul and Joyce Heil all reviewed the manuscript at different stages and their feedback made it better. Barbara Juliani and the staff of New Growth Press did a great job guiding it to publication. Patric Knaak offered excellent editorial feedback and also served as a valuable encouragement through the process. Lindsay Kimball made the discussion questions better than I would have written on my own. My Serge Kibuye teammates have walked with me for many years now, and our shared experiences and conversations form the matrix for the book's content. Everyone can see I am obviously indebted to the many great writers I have quoted. I am thankful for their talent and their labor, which is a gift to so many. My parents taught me the importance of walking with those in need and gave me an abiding love of Scripture. In the end, Rachel is my first and best editor. Every reader should thank her for ensuring that my thoughts are comprehensible to someone who is not married to me. Without her support, I wouldn't have ever tried to put this book together.

Endnotes

CHAPTER 1: BROTHER'S KEEPER

1. David Brooks, "The Ultimate Spoiler Alert" (commencement address at Dartmouth University, Hanover, NH, June 14, 2015). Transcript accessed at https://news.dartmouth.edu/news/2015/06/david-brooks -commencement-address.

2. Genesis 4:9

3. Ephesians 4:15

4. Luke 10:25–37

5. J. R. R. Tolkien, *The Tolkien Reader* (New York: Ballantine, 1966), 68 and 72.

CHAPTER 2: INSUFFICIENCY

1. Shane Claiborne, Enuma Okoro, and Jonathan Wilson-Hartgrove, *Common Prayer: A Liturgy for Ordinary Radicals* (Grand Rapids: Zondervan Publishing House, 2010), 241.

2. Names of patients are routinely changed to protect their identity. Additionally, smaller details (such as what they are wearing) may not be remembered one hundred percent accurately. They are included for the purpose of portraying their personhood and the circumstances with the full dignity of reality.

3. 2 Corinthians 12:7–10

4. Ibid.

CHAPTER 3: PROMISE

1. Frederick Buechner, *Now and Then: A Memoir of Vocation* (New York: HarperCollins, 1991), 109.

2. Revelation 21:5

3. Andrew Peterson, "Dancing in the Minefields," 2010, track 2 on *Counting Stars,* Centricity Music, digital album.

4. Genesis 12:1–7ff. The three major elements of God's promises to Abraham (descendants, land, blessing to all nations) are all present in Genesis 12, even though some of the biblical images used here are not used until later.

5. Genesis 15:5

6. Genesis 22:17

7. Genesis 15:2
8. Genesis 21:6
9. Matthew 5:4
10. Isaiah 59:1
11. Deuteronomy 10:18
12. Philippians 4:9
13. Hebrews 13:5 (NIV)
14. 2 Corinthians 4:16 (NIV)

CHAPTER 4: DESPAIR

1. Andrew Peterson, "MONEY, Part 4: Little Things Matter" last modified September 7, 2010, https://rabbitroom.com/2010/09/money-part-4-little -things-matter.
2. Michael Card, *A Sacred Sorrow: Reaching Out to God in the Lost Language of Lament* (Colorado Springs: NavPress, 2014), 55.
3. Job 30:20
4. Psalm 34:18
5. Lamentations 2:5
6. Psalm 88:14
7. Psalm 44:24
8. 1 Corinthians 15:54–55

CHAPTER 5: HOPE

1. Romans 5:5 (RSV)
2. Proverbs 13:12
3. Matthew 1:23, which references Isaiah 7:14.
4. John 20:19

CHAPTER 6: TIME

1. Wendell Berry, *This Day: Collected & New Sabbath Poems 1979-2013* (Berkeley, CA: Counterpoint, 2013), 141 (Poem I of 1993).
2. Proverbs 8:22–31
3. Psalm 119:126
4. Galatians 4:4
5. Berry, 132 (Poem IV of 1992).

CHAPTER 7: ORDINARY

1. Compiled by Sarah Arthur, *At the Still Point: A Literary Guide to Prayer in Ordinary Time* (Brewster, MA: Paraclete Press, 2011).
2. Ecclesiastes 2:24
3. Proverbs 5:18

4. Zechariah 3:10

5. Berry, 28 (Poem IV of 1980).

6. John 1:5 (NIV)

7. Matthew 13:31–33

8. Walt Wangerin Jr., *The Book of the Dun Cow* (New York: Harper & Row, 1978), 24.

9. Robert Farrar Capon, *The Supper of the Lamb: A Culinary Reflection* (New York: Random House, 2002), 99.

CHAPTER 8: HAUNTED

1. The Talmud, 303.

2. Galatians 2:20

3. Matthew 25:40

4. Matthew 5:42

5. Timothy Keller, "Hope for the Poor: The Gospel, Hope, and the World," October 4, 2009, Redeemer Presbyterian Church, New York, sermon transcript, http://storage.cloversites.com/highpeakfellowship/documents/Hope_For_The_Poor.pdf. Both the illustration of Oskar Schindler and the discussion of 1 John 3 in this context are adapted from this sermon.

6. 1 John 3:20 (NIV)

7. 1 John 3:1 (NIV)

CHAPTER 9: PRAYER

1. Philip Yancey, *Prayer: Does It Make Any Difference?* (Grand Rapids: Zondervan, 2006), 82.

2. Mark 12:41–44

3. Ole Hallesby, *Prayer* (Minneapolis: Augsburg Fortress, 1994), 18–28.

4. John 2:3

5. 2 Corinthians 12:9

6. James 5:16 (NIV)

7. Mark 10:47

8. Luke 11:5–10

9. Luke 18:1–8

10. Mark 7:24–30

11. Frederick Buechner, *Wishful Thinking: A Seeker's ABC* (New York: HarperOne, 1993), 87.

CHAPTER 10: MYSTERY

1. Marilynne Robinson, *Lila* (New York: Farrar, Straus, and Giroux, 2014), loc. 434–435, Kindle.

2. Isaiah 6:4–11

CHAPTER 11: SUFFERING

1. Nicholas Wolterstorff, *Lament for a Son* (Grand Rapids: Eerdmans, 1987), 90.
2. Card, *A Sacred Sorrow*, 43.
3. Card, *A Sacred Sorrow*, 17.
4. Frederick Buechner, *Peculiar Treasures: A Biblical Who's Who* (New York: Harper & Row, 1979), 68–89.
5. Paul Gerhardt (source attributed to Bernard of Clairvaux), "O Sacred Head, Now Wounded," Hymn #178 in *The Hymnal for Worship & Celebration* (Waco, TX: Word Music, 1986).
6. Frederick Buechner, *Wishful Thinking: A Seeker's ABC* (New York: HarperOne, 1993), 117.
7. This was a personal memory from hearing Steve Saint speak at the Global Missions Health Conference at Southeast Christian Church in Louisville, KY, ca. 2011.

CHAPTER 12: CONSOLATION

1. Donald McNeill, Douglas Morrison, and Henri Nouwen, *Compassion: A Reflection on the Christian Life* (New York: Image, Doubleday, 1982), 4.
2. 2 Corinthians 1:4
3. Victor Hugo, *Les Misérables* (Project Gutenberg ebook, French language version, public domain), loc. 4310–4313, Kindle.
4. Robinson, loc. 3793–3794, Kindle.
5. Job 13:4–5
6. 2 Samuel 12:15–23
7. 2 Samuel 18:32–19:8
8. John 11:17–35
9. Luke 10:38–42
10. Romans 12:15
11. Matthew 5:4
12. Psalm 34:18
13. Paul Miller, *A Praying Life: Connecting with God in a Distracting World* (Colorado Springs, CO: NavPress, 2009), 180–81.
14. Romans 13:10
15. J. R. R. Tolkien, *The Return of the King: The Lord of the Rings, Part 3* (New York: Ballantine, 1965), 242.

CHAPTER 13: RESURRECTION

1. Berry, 38 (Poem IV of 1982).
2. Hebrews 11:19
3. N. T. Wright, *Surprised by Hope: Rethinking Heaven, the Resurrection, and the Mission of the Church* (New York: HarperOne, 2008), 256–57.

4. 1 Thessalonians 4:13
5. John 11:25–26
6. 1 Corinthians 15:26
7. Psalm 139:6
8. 1 Corinthians 15:51–54 (NIV)
9. 1 Corinthians 15:47–49

CHAPTER 14: DARKNESS AND LIGHT

1. Gerard Manley Hopkins, *Hopkins: Poems and Prose,* Everyman's Library Pocket Poet Series (New York: Alfred A. Knopf, Inc, 1995), 86. Excerpt is from "That Nature Is a Heraclitean Fire and of the Comfort of the Resurrection."
2. Frederick Buechner, *Godric: A Novel* (New York: HarperCollins, 1983), 96.
3. Stanley Hauerwas, *God, Medicine, and Suffering* (Grand Rapids, MI: Eerdmans, 1990), loc. 588–90, Kindle.
4. Matthew 5:14
5. John 8:12

CHAPTER 15: REDEMPTION

1. Fanny Crosby, "Give Me Jesus," Hymn 443 in *The Hymnal for Worship & Celebration* (Waco: Word Music, 1986).
2. Ibid.
3. Revelation 21:5
4. Mark 5:1–20
5. Mark 5:19
6. Genesis 21:3–6
7. Romans 8:20–22
8. Revelation 21:1–3
9. Revelation 22:2
10. "Redeem," dictionary.com, accessed February 13, 2019, https://www.dictionary.com/browse/redeem.
11. Crosby, "Give Me Jesus."

EPILOGUE: PROMISES IN THE DARK

1. Matthew 3:7
2. Luke 7:18–23
3. Luke 7:23
4. Psalm 137:4
5. Isaiah 59:1; John 5:17 (NIV).
6. Alexsandr Solzhenitsyn, *The Gulag Archipelago, 1918–1956* (New York: Harper & Row, 1974), 168.
7. 2 Corinthians 4:16

mission
propelled by good news

At Serge we believe that mission begins through the gospel of Jesus Christ bringing God's grace into the lives of believers. This good news also sustains and empowers us to cross nations and cultures to bring the gospel of grace to those whom God is calling to himself.

As a cross-denominational, reformed sending agency with more than two hundred missionaries and twenty-five teams in five continents, we are always looking for people who are ready to take the next step in sharing Christ through:

- **Short-term Teams:** One- to two-week trips oriented around serving overseas ministries while equipping the local church for mission

- **Internships:** Eight-week to nine-month opportunities to learn about missions through serving with our overseas ministry teams

- **Apprenticeships:** Intensive twelve- to twenty-four-month training and ministry opportunities for those discerning their call to cross-cultural ministry

- **Career:** One- to five-year appointments designed to nurture you for a lifetime of ministry

 Grace at the Fray   **Visit us online at: serge.org/mission**

www.newgrowthpress.com